THE AUTHORITY GUIDE TO
PRESENTING AND PUBLIC SPEAKING

How to deliver engaging and effective
business presentations

STEVE BUSTIN

The Authority Guide to Presenting and Public Speaking

How to deliver engaging and effective business presentations

© Steve Bustin

ISBN 978-1-909116-75-7

eISBN 978-1-909116-76-4

Published in 2016 by Authority Guides

authorityguides.co.uk

Image credit:
Figure 3: Roger Harrop
Figure 5: Open Hardware Summit
Figures 7 and 8: Click-Click Jim

Printed in the United Kingdom.

For John, my rock.

Be still when you have nothing to say;
when genuine passion moves you, say
what you've got to say, and say it hot.

D. H. Lawrence

Credits, acknowledgements and thanks

This book could not have been written without help and input from a number of people:

- My husband John Williams, not only for his support, encouragement and patience, but also for proofreading, critiquing and making suggestions.

- Sue Richardson of SRA Books who offered me the opportunity to get involved with the Authority Guides and whose expert advice and personal support has been invaluable.

- Roger Harrop, one of the UK's top business speakers (www.rogerharrop.com), who has kindly been acting as my mentor through the Professional Speaking Association (PSA), and who let me use one of his slides in this book.

- Niels Brabandt, Anthony Stears and also Felix Schweikert, my mastermind buddies, for cajoling and encouraging in equal measure.

- Simon Powell who allowed me to adapt and develop an earlier version of his fishbone template.

- A credit to photographer Click-Click Jim (photo in Figures 7 and 8) and Open Hardware Summit for the Creative Commons licensed image in Figure 5.

- All those who answered the survey featured in Appendix 1 – thank you for your honest answers.

Contents

There are only two types of speakers in the world. 1. The nervous and 2. Liars.

Mark Twain

Introduction

Presentations are now a fact of life. For many people a slightly unpleasant fact of life, a bit like a trip to the dentist or a day of enforced jollity with some distant relatives. Something to be endured, but you'll be left with a vague sense of satisfaction and achievement at having survived it. So the fact that you've picked up this book suggests that (a) you know you're going to have to make a presentation at some point and (b) you'd like some help to make it as successful – and even pleasant – an experience as possible.

You'll often hear people cite research which states that most of us are more scared of public speaking or presenting than we are of death. Really? Twenty minutes speaking to an audience is a less appealing prospect than an ever-after of absolute nothingness? Yikes. You must have seen some terrible presentations in your time.

I'm one of those strange people who enjoy presenting and speaking in public. I always have. I compèred my first event when I was 11 (a Burns supper at my primary school in Scotland, despite the fact I'm English) and won my first award for speaking in public when I was 13. I haven't shut up since. Now I do it (and teach others to do it) for a living. I enjoy knowing that I can take an audience on a journey as I share my expertise, experience and stories, which is what this book is all about.

The feedback I normally get when I speak or present (and we'll look shortly at whether those two terms are interchangeable) is that audience members like my confidence, my engagement with them and the fact they get tools, tips and other 'takeaways' they really can take away and use immediately. Those are the key things I want to share with you in this Authority Guide. By the end of this book you will have the tools and tips you need to give confident, engaging and effective presentations that leave your audience not only awake, but positively enthusiastic, meeting both your – and their – objectives.

Why do we give presentations and speeches?

We give presentations not as a form of punishment for the presenter or audience, but because they work. Human to human interaction is at the heart of how we learn, share, communicate and promulgate information, skills and knowledge – and also often how we entertain and engage.

Yes, you can read books (starting with this one, obviously), watch videos, take part in webinars or conference calls, engage on social media or listen to a podcast, but there's a reason why we still have meetings, attend conferences, pitch for work, invite people to present to us or seek out speakers that 'speak' to us on all sorts of levels. As humans we respond in a very basic and deep way to listening to the human voice, especially if that voice is talking our language and giving us information that is pertinent and useful to us.

Presenting and public speaking are now *essential* business skills. If you're a business leader you need to be able to address your staff, inspire and motivate them to take your organisation forward. You may also be asked to represent your organisation or even industry sector by speaking at conferences and events.

If you're a business owner you need to be able to pitch and promote your business to potential clients and customers and to speak at networking events. Public speaking is also an essential part of a modern business development strategy.

If you're an employee and looking to develop your career, presentations are a great way to raise your profile and highlight your skills to your peers and bosses. Many job interviews (especially at senior levels) now include giving a presentation as part of the selection process.

You may even be looking to turn speaking into your career, flying around the world to speak for huge fees at conferences and events, sharing your vision for the world and with the world. It's a fun way to earn a living – if not quite as glamorous or as well paid as you may hope.

Saying 'I don't want or need to present' is no longer an option. If you're running a business or you're part of an organisation, it's a skill set you need to develop, hone and practise. That's where this book comes in.

What's changed about presentations?

Presentations have changed because *we* have changed and business has changed. Our attention span is shorter. The demands on our time are greater, but our appetite for new information, ideas and inspiration has also grown.

Presentations now tend to be shorter, more interactive and more engaging than they used to be. The days of someone talking to a deck of slides covered in bullet points are, thankfully (hopefully?), almost over.

A few words on terminology

There are lots of different words commonly used to describe the topic at hand – presentation, speech, public speaking and pitching, for example.

There are distinctions to be drawn between some of these terms, but for the purposes of this book we'll assume that they are all pretty interchangeable, as when you present or pitch you are giving a speech – and when you are public speaking you are presenting. Therefore I will primarily use the word 'presentation' as a catch-all term, as this is what most of us give in a business context, whether that's presenting in an internal meeting or presenting at a major international conference.

Also, I'll be using the word 'audience' quite a bit too, as any presentation has to have an audience (talking to yourself in a meeting room isn't to be recommended), whether that's an audience of three or four or an audience of 2,500 in a conference hall. The number of people in the audience will affect the way you present (don't stand up and bellow at four people, please), but shouldn't make any difference to the time, care and attention you put into preparing and delivering your presentation. All audiences deserve to hear and see the best possible presentation.

How (and when) to use this book

This book can be used in two ways. First, read it from beginning to end in the traditional way as it follows the chronological order of the steps needed to give a great presentation and be a great presenter. Start at the beginning and by the end you'll understand why many of the steps need to be followed in a particular order.

Second, it's also designed to be a reference book, to be dipped in to when you need a refresher or some ideas on a certain element of presenting. Even experienced presenters and speakers sometimes want to try something new or refresh their approach. Certain chapters are likely to be useful resources when you need inspiration to avoid getting stuck in a presentation rut.

A good orator is pointed and impassioned.

Marcus T. Cicero

The anatomy of a good presentation

What constitutes a good or bad presentation?

Before we start looking at your presentation, let's think about other people's presentations, the way they make those presentations and what we can learn from them.

What constitutes a good presentation? Everyone will have their own specific likes and dislikes, but common responses to this question include:

- Interesting content
- Useful content
- Entertaining or engaging
- Relevant to me
- Easy voice to listen to
- Confident presenter
- Good stage presence
- Great slides
- No slides
- Short/succinct – no padding

Ask people what constitutes a bad presentation and the list can go on for days, but the responses that tend to top the list include:

- Dull
- Not relevant
- Too long
- Death by PowerPoint
- Nervous presenter
- No structure, hard to follow
- No obvious takeaways
- Starts with an apology – and goes downhill from there

What's interesting is that the first list is predominantly about the audience and what they wanted to get out of it: 'I found it useful', 'I found it relevant', 'I liked the slides'. The 'bad' list, however, errs more towards the presenter and their material or style: dull, nervous, no takeaways and so on.

Clearly you want your presentation to fit into the first list not the second and you need to take steps to address the factors that appear in both lists. We'll talk more in the next chapter about understanding what your audience wants to get out of your presentation. Your job as presenter is to set out to deliver a 'good' presentation as much by addressing the potential negatives as by ensuring you meet the positive criteria. Both lists are within your control.

What constitutes a good or bad presenter?

Who do you rate as a good presenter? Think about your own organisation or events you've attended. Whose presentations and speeches stick in your mind as being particularly good?

Why were they memorable? What about presenters from the wider world – politicians, business leaders and the like? Who do you rate and what makes them good presenters?

When I am coaching people on their presentations and ask them to undertake this exercise, they will often come up with the name of their boss, then big names such as Barack Obama, Richard Branson, Steve Jobs or Margaret Thatcher.

Obviously everyone's list of criteria for what makes these people great speakers will be different, but the common responses include:

- Engaging
- Entertaining/uses humour
- Makes it feel like they're talking directly to you
- Doesn't use slides
- Has gravitas
- Varied vocal tone
- Speaks slowly and clearly
- Passionate about their topic
- Has something of value to say

Although you probably didn't assign every one of these traits to all the speakers you listed (and often political views can colour our views of whether a politician is a great speaker or not), these are the factors that most people agree make someone a good speaker.

Exercise

Now run the opposite exercise, looking at presenters you remember as being particularly poor. What traits did they all have?

Top tip

Get into the habit of critiquing the speakers you see in action, whether you're in a meeting listening to a colleague, at a conference watching a keynote speaker or seeing someone on TV. When you warm to a speaker, note what it is that's attracting and engaging you. Is it the way they speak? The visual aids they're using? Or the fact that they're talking your language and making it completely targeted and relevant to you?

Perhaps more importantly, when you find yourself switching off during a presentation, ask yourself why. Was it the speaker or their content? Is the content irrelevant or are you lost because it's badly structured? Is the speaker droning on in a soporific way?

When you've noted the good or bad traits (and many speakers will display a mix of both), think about how you can either follow their example – or avoid their mistakes. How can you emulate the good speakers and learn what not to do from the poor ones?

But – and it's a big but – don't set out to copy the good speakers. It's important that you find your own presenting style and hone that.

Find your style

When I'm coaching speakers and presenters, people often ask me to train them to speak just like me. I have to explain that I can't do that. What I can do is train them to speak like them – to find their own personal presentation style and make that the best it can be.

Exercise

Write down a list of what you think your strengths and weaknesses are as a presenter. List three of each, although it's worth remembering that most people find it far easier to come up with weaknesses than strengths, as we're our own harshest critics. Have a look at that list and have a think about how you can build on the strengths and address the weaknesses. If you're struggling to identify your strengths and/or weaknesses, ask two or three people who have seen you present what they think.

Even experienced speakers have weaknesses. It doesn't necessarily make them bad speakers, but it means they have traits that need addressing.

For instance, I think my strengths as a presenter are:

- People tell me I'm warm and engaging when I present – someone once said I 'sparkle' when I step on stage

- My content is very practical – my adage is that if an audience member doesn't go away with at least one thing they can take back to their desk and do differently tomorrow, I've failed

- I rarely use slides unless I think they'll really enhance a presentation for my audience. Audience members at events with lots of speakers have commented that my presentation stood out more because I didn't use slides

I think my weaknesses are:

- I know I can talk too fast, especially when I'm really excited about something or if I'm nervous
- I sometimes try to cram too much content into a presentation, which means audiences can be a bit overwhelmed or my key messages get lost
- I can occasionally get stuck in a slightly stilted delivery if I'm speaking words I've used over and over again in the past

Top tip

By knowing my strengths I build on them and use them to their maximum advantage when I'm presenting. By identifying my weaknesses I address them and reduce the risk of repeating them.

Knowing my strengths and addressing my weaknesses has helped me to hone my personal presentation style. My aim is to come across as warm; friendly and approachable; professional; with gravitas; and as an expert in my topics. Feedback from audiences and other speakers leads me to believe I'm getting it about right.

Exercise

Having identified your strengths and weaknesses as a presenter, how do you want to come across when presenting? What would you like your personal presenting style to be? Whose style do you respect and might want to emulate (but not copy)? What might need to change in your current presentation style to help you move towards that goal?

A few words about 'passion'

I have a love/hate relationship with the term 'passion'.

Top tip

If you have to tell me you're passionate (for instance in your biography or when someone introduces you before you give a presentation), you're not. Passion should be intrinsic to who you are, what you do and the way you do it, and it should 'sing out' when you're presenting. If you have to point out how passionate you are, you clearly aren't passionate enough for me to notice.

Having said that, passion is incredibly important in a presentation and as a presenter. When critiquing both business and famous speakers, it's a word that comes up time and time again as not just a positive criterion, but also a requirement of a good speaker.

If you don't have passion for your topic or your content, why on earth should your audience? If your passion for your topic is evident (even if you know your topic is a little 'dry'), then your audience is far more likely to remain engaged. Your passion can show through in your expertise, your eagerness to communicate that expertise and the energy with which you throw yourself into your presentation. The next time you see someone speak, ask yourself: Does this person have passion for their topic and if so, how can I tell?

Exercise

If you're not sure if you're presenting with passion, try speaking for 60 seconds on a topic you really are passionate about – your favourite sport or team, your family, your hobby, anything you can really get passionate about. How does that feel? What were you doing with your body and voice that communicated passion? Can you take that feeling and those actions and apply them to a business presentation?

Top tip

If you're not passionate about your topic, don't expect your audience to be.

Setting objectives for your presentation

There's an old adage that 'a good presentation doesn't start on the podium, it starts in the preparation', and it's a good one to follow. Think of a presentation like an iceberg. What the audience sees is only the tip of your work, as the bulk of your work is out of sight, hidden in the time you spent preparing and rehearsing your presentation. Making it look easy is hard work.

So, how do you start planning your presentation? If you start by sitting staring at a blank PowerPoint slide, that's the wrong way to start. If you start by looking at the cursor flashing at the top of a Word document, that's the wrong way to start. If you start with a blank piece of paper and a pen, you're half way there – but if you start writing your content, that's the wrong way to start.

Before you start writing your content, let alone designing slides, your starting point should be setting some objectives for your presentation. Two sets of objectives, in fact. Some for yourself and some for your audience.

Top tip

Setting clear objectives at this early stage gives you clarity about the content you need to prepare and deliver in order to meet your (and your audience's) objectives.

Your objectives also give you something to measure against. Once you've written your presentation and built your slides, you can go back to your objectives and think, 'If I deliver this content, will I meet my objectives?' After you've delivered your presentation, you can go back to your objectives again and ask yourself, 'Did I meet my objectives? Did my audience meet theirs? If not, what do I need to change before I give this or a similar presentation again in order to meet those objectives next time?'

Step 1: setting objectives for yourself

Start the planning process by asking yourself these questions:

- Why am I giving this presentation?
- What do I want to get out of it?
- What do I want it to achieve?

If you struggle to answer these questions, you're going to struggle to write and deliver an effective presentation.

So what might be your objectives for a presentation? They can be both professional and personal, and for any given presentation you may well have a combination of both.

Let's start with some examples of professional objectives. You might want your presentation to:

- give your audience new knowledge, skills or updated information
- motivate or inspire your audience
- change behaviour – you want your audience to go away and do something differently
- change thinking or opinions
- get your audience to do something specific, such as visit a website, download something, buy a product, buy a ticket,

invest, spread the word, call you, follow you on social media and so on

- persuade the audience to hire you or buy your product or service in a pitch situation.

You can also have personal objectives for your presentation. You might want your presentation to:

- impress your boss or colleagues
- help to get you a promotion or a new job
- help to raise your profile within an organisation
- help to establish yourself as an opinion former or thought leader
- give you a new string to your bow.

Any or all of these would be great objectives and you'll probably be able to come up with plenty more.

Step 2: setting objectives for your audience

A presentation isn't just about you and what you want. It's all too easy to go into a presentation without really thinking about what your audience wants to get out of it. Why are they there? What's in it for them? Don't fall into the trap of assuming that they are there for the same reasons as you. Put yourself in their shoes. What's uppermost in their mind as you take the stage? Is it 'I need to learn new stuff' or 'I hope this isn't dull'? It's probably a mix of both.

Just like you, a member of your audience will have both professional and personal objectives. An audience member's professional objectives might include:

- Learning something new
- Being able to do their job better by gaining new skills

- Understanding their place within the organisation or on a particular project

- Feeling part of a team

- Finding out what they need to do next

Their personal objectives can be very different – and quite revealing. These might include:

- Not being bored. No audience member sits there wanting to be bored. They want to be engaged, entertained even. This is probably top of their agenda – and if you don't meet this objective, you're never going to meet any of your own objectives as you'll lose your audience very fast indeed.

- Finding something useful in your content. Is there something they can take away and use right now that will make their life easier or help them to do their job better?

- Knowing how to make their bonus or other goal more quickly and easily.

- Impressing the boss just by being there, asking pertinent questions or proving they know more than the person giving the presentation.

- Boosting their career prospects by networking and being seen at the right events.

An audience member's objectives will usually be driven by self-interest: What's in it for me, personally *and* professionally? So *your* objectives should also be driven by exactly the same self-interest: What's in it for me? What do I want to get out of it?

Example

You've been tasked by your boss with presenting the latest quarterly sales figures to the sales team, at a large team meeting, with the instruction to motivate them to achieve better sales.

1   What might your objectives be?

Your professional objectives might include:

- Make sure everyone understands the sales figures
- Make sure everyone knows what the targets are for the next quarter
- Encourage team bonding
- Lead the generation of ideas by the team on how to reach those targets

Your personal objectives might include:

- Impressing your boss who delegated this task to you
- Impressing the team and lining yourself up for future promotion
- Being seen as 'an ideas person'
- Ensuring your place in the team is safe and you are respected by your colleagues

2   What might your audience's objectives be?

Their objectives might include:

- What role have I played in these figures? Is my job safe? I want reassurance.
- How do I earn more commission? I want tactics and tools.

- Please don't let this be as boring as every other sales figures presentation.

- How do I make sure the team is pulling together? I want to see evidence of leadership.

- I want to be asked to make this presentation next time.

These are a mix of personal and professional objectives. It's often harder to separate the two when considering someone else's self-interest.

Now we've identified both our own and our audience's objectives for this presentation, we can start to prepare our content accordingly. Just because your priority is communicating the sales figures, it doesn't mean that the audience is focused on those figures in the same way. Chances are they're more focused on their role within the team, the security of their job and, more importantly, how they earn their commission. If you fail to address those objectives, they'll leave your presentation feeling short-changed as they didn't get what they wanted or needed. Thus your objectives will fail as you won't get the results you need from the individuals or the team.

Exercise

Take a presentation you are either about to give or one you have given recently and try setting some objectives for it. Identify two or three professional and two or three personal objectives for yourself – what you want to get out of it – then set two or three objectives for your audience – what do they want to get out of it?

Creating your content

Now you know what your presentation needs to achieve, you can finally start thinking about the content you need to prepare in order to meet those objectives. There are two main steps to this process. Firstly, creating content and secondly, structuring your content (which we'll come to in the next chapter).

Here are some techniques you can use to create content. (You'll probably find one or two of these feel right and others you just think 'what is he on about?' but that's fine – finding the right tool to stimulate your thinking is what matters.)

The good old-fashioned brain dump

Sometimes you just need to empty your brain to collect all those disparate thoughts that are banging around in there. You need to transfer those thoughts from brain to page and this is where personal taste comes into play. Are you a pen and paper advocate, a keen mind-mapper or an Evernote (www.evernote.com) evangelist?

Set a timer on your phone and concentrate on writing down as many words or phrases to do with the topic as you can within that time. Write down the ideas that are already in your head.

Don't edit at this stage – even the vaguest or most tangential thought can turn into useful content at a later date.

Once you've written that list, leave it. Put the kettle on. Then come back to the list, add anything else that immediately occurs to you and then go through each point you've listed and try to spin something off that: How could I illustrate this? What story could I tell about this? What else would an audience need to know about this point?

Depending on how much time you've got, you can come back to this list and keep adding to it, but eventually you need to start editing. Count how many points you've listed. I normally work on needing half the number of points than I've got minutes to present – that is, I need 15 points, comments or stories for a 30 minute presentation, although I often end up reducing it so it's less than half that number again, as it can actually take several minutes to make each point or tell each story.

Take out any points that you don't think really fit with your topic or that you no longer need and start ranking the others by how keen you are to include them. Do you have a favourite story or piece of research? Is there a point you're not 100 per cent convinced is relevant? Once you've got your list of ranked points you should have more than enough ideas for your presentation and you're ready to move on to structuring those into content.

Exercise

Try the 'brain dump' exercise as outlined above for a presentation you're preparing. Note how many ideas and points you came up with.

FAQs

Another good way to create content is to draw up a list of FAQs (frequently asked questions) about your topic. Make a list of all the things you think your audience might want to ask about the topic. Put yourself in their shoes and write down their likely questions. This could be anything from asking you to define certain key words you're likely to use during your presentation to asking questions such as:

- Why is this relevant to me?
- How do I use this in my everyday job or life?
- What research is there to back this up?
- How has this worked in the past?
- Does it work?

List as many FAQs as you can and then set about answering them, writing answers in longhand if necessary, or jotting down a few bullet points about how you would go about answering them. These answers become your content.

You can even take this beyond a theoretical exercise and ask people what their questions would be on a certain topic – even ask your intended audience what they'd like to know, if you have a way of interacting with them. You can also ask the person who has asked you to present what questions they think the audience will have, or how about opening it up on social media, posting a status update such as: 'If you could ask any question about [this topic], what would it be?'

Exercise

Run the FAQs exercise for a presentation you've got coming up. Note how many ideas and points you came up with.

Research – what have other people said?

If you're not sure what to say about a topic, read around it a bit and discover what other people have said. Do you agree or disagree with them? Do you have different ideas or a different approach? What inspires you in what they've said or what made you laugh or got you angry? This should be enough stimulus to trigger your own thoughts on the topic.

A word of warning about this method: while research is an important part of knowing your topic, this doesn't give you carte blanche to copy or use other people's material. You may well find research you can cite, quotes you can use or ways of presenting data that you can emulate – but you *must* credit someone else's work or materials and they must make up a relatively small part of your presentation (less than 10 per cent) as people want to hear your take on the topic, not a rehash of someone else's. You're using other people's thinking as inspiration and a jumping off point for your own thinking, not as a direct source of content.

Exercise

Run the research exercise as outlined above. Note how many ideas and points you came up with.

Which of the three exercises generated the most ideas and points for you?

Why structuring your content is vital

Whether your presentation is 5 minutes long or 90 minutes long, you need to give it structure. It needs to have clear sections so that your audience knows where they are and can follow along throughout your time in front of them. It also needs clear 'signposts' so the audience knows which part of the presentation you're currently in and can process the information you deliver accordingly.

Don't fall into the 'stream of consciousness' presentation trap, where you talk around and about your topic, heading off on random tangents, leaving your audience wondering where you are, what you're talking about or the point you're trying to make.

Beginning, middle and end

There's a much-quoted adage that in any presentation you should 'tell them what you're going to tell them, tell it to them, then tell them what you've just told them'. Someone recently tried to assure me that it was an old army saying, but it is in fact from the father of rhetoric himself, Aristotle, albeit in a slightly more soundbitey form.

Aristotle's words still hold true. Your opening sets the scene and previews what you're going to say in your central section, which you then present with the bulk of your content, and the closing section summarises and recaps what you've just said.

> ### Top tip
>
> There are three main sections of any presentation that you need to build into your structure. Simply put, the opening, the content-rich middle section and the closing. The middle section then needs some structure of its own (more on that shortly), but the presentation as a whole needs to follow that basic shape. Beginning, middle and end. It's a format that's been around as long as we've told stories, and for good reason. It works.

Your opening and closing sections play a far more important role than just outlining and recapping, however. If you don't get your opening and closing sections right, all your hard work will have been in vain and people will leave remembering very little – or remembering certain bits for the wrong reason. Let's explore why.

Open with a bang, not a whimper

Irrespective of how long your presentation is, your opening section serves a number of purposes:

- It tells your audience what's in it for them, that is, why they should listen. Your opening should let the audience know that what's about to follow is not only important, but is relevant and useful to them.

- It tells your audience why you are the right person to be talking about this topic – that is, your credibility, which reinforces why the audience should stop checking their emails and listen to you.

- It sets the tone. Not only is this presentation going to be important and relevant, but it's going to be interesting or thought provoking or high energy or funny or critical or of monetary value to them. (On that last point – many employees, especially those in sales, are really motivated by money, so make sure you tell these audiences very quickly that this presentation is going to help them make their bonus or commission faster/more easily/tomorrow, and they're going to listen intently right from the outset.)

You should open in the way you mean to go on – don't start high energy then suddenly go quiet when you get to your content, or start with lots of humour and interaction then go into reading your script once your opening section is done.

- It grabs your audience and makes a good first impression. Spoiler alert: an audience isn't always terribly interested in what you've got to say. They may be in the audience because they have to be, because they want to hear one of the other speakers or because there was a free lunch. They may even have come especially to listen to you, but have been bored to the point of stupor by the previous speaker. Your opening is a chance to wake them up, shake them up, pull their focus and make sure they're listening.

That's not a lot to do in an opening section that might only last a couple of minutes, is it?

We've all seen presenters open badly. 'Hello, my name is Steve and today I'm going to talk to you about blah, blah, blah.' Just dull. Or 'I've got lots of figures to show you today that are going to be a bit dull so just stick with me…' If even the presenter thinks they're dull, what chance do the audience have? Or how about 'I'm really sorry, but I'm not very good at presenting and I'm not sure whether my slides are going to work and I'm afraid I've got a bit of a sore throat and my voice is a bit croaky.'

Top tip

Never start with an apology – it immediately sets you off on a negative note. You might be falling apart inside, but try to exude confidence. If you're positive, your audience will be positive – but they'll pick up on negative 'energy' very quickly and switch off.

What makes a strong opening?

Here are some ideas you can try.

- **Questions** make a great opening because they can get people thinking about the topic at hand. You need to decide, however, whether you're you're asking a rhetorical question, or a direct question that you want the audience to respond to.

  Make it clear which you're asking and whether you want a response. You don't want a stony silence after your opening question – but nor do you want someone trying to answer your rhetorical question and crashing into your opening section. Personally I always prefer to ask a direct question as I like to get audience interaction started as early as possible.

- **A straw poll**. A variant on the question, it can be useful to sound out the mood or knowledge of the room on a certain topic. 'Quick show of hands – how many people have done/read/seen X?' Be prepared to adjust your content based on their answer.

Top tip

As you ask for a show of hands, raise your hand too. Audience members hate being the first person to raise their hand, in case they're the only one to do so. By raising your hand as you ask the question you give them permission to do so. For the same reason, always try to open with a yes/no question to which most of the audience will say yes, so they feel it's a positive group experience.

- **A quote, phrase or saying**. This can be delivered verbally or put up on a slide. You're looking for something that is pertinent to the topic and will set your audience thinking. Always credit it to whoever said it (and check who said it thoroughly; don't believe everything you find on Wikipedia).

A good spin on this that I've seen work very effectively is to put up a controversial quote or something that the audience won't expect, but without an attribution. Ask the audience who said it, and then reveal that it's you that is saying it – it's a great way to introduce your key message with impact.

- **An image**. If you're using slides, an interesting, quirky, funny or impactful image can make a great opening by setting the tone and sending a message. It can even be up on the screen before you start, letting delegates study and ponder it.

An important note: make sure you're legally allowed to use your chosen image and don't just download the first one you find from Google Image search as it may well be under copyright. Both Google and Flickr allow you to narrow down image searches to find images available under what are known as Creative Commons licenses, which are used by photographers and image creators to allow different types of use, including commercial and public uses. Google 'creative commons license' for more information on how this works.

The safest (and often most engaging) method is to take and use your own images. Even shots taken on most smartphones are perfectly good enough quality to blow up to full screen on a slide. Alternatively, commission a creative photographer to take shots for you to illustrate certain themes or stories.

- **A video**. A well-crafted video (even just shot using your phone) or well-chosen clip can really kick off your presentation with impact. Keep it to a maximum of 90 seconds (people are here to listen to you, not watch videos after all) and make sure you have audio facilities wherever you're presenting.

Another important note: as with images, don't infringe copyright. Make your own videos or search for those with Creative Commons licenses on YouTube. Just because it's been posted by someone other than the original creator (such as one of the major film companies or broadcasters) doesn't mean you won't be infringing copyright by using it, especially if you're playing it in public and/or making money from using it. Some film and TV companies will grant a licence for usage if you ask them in writing, although they may charge a licence fee.

- **A joke or something humorous**. Laughter is incredibly engaging, but can be a tricky one to pull off as a joke that falls flat will leave the whole room feeling awkward. There's nothing wrong with preparing a humorous remark in advance and practise saying it out loud so you don't fluff it. You don't need a gag or joke ('knock knock...') as a lot of the most natural humour comes from either a shared experience or by pointing out something interesting, unusual or amusing in the room.

But (and it's an important but), jokes and humour must be carefully handled and should be context sensitive. Never tell a joke that makes someone the victim or fall guy. Never use humour that is any way sexist, racist or homophobic or could be construed as offensive and never make assumptions about who is or isn't in your audience and what they'll find funny.

Certainly only open with something humorous when delivering a presentation that allows for it. For instance, if you're about to announce cuts or redundancies, opening with a hilarious gag is a seriously bad move.

Finally, don't be scared to let your slides take the load when it comes to humour. If you find a pertinent or relevant funny picture or cartoon (copyright allowing) you can put that on your opening slide to get the laugh. If you see people whip out their phones and take a photo of your slide to share, you know it engaged them!

- **Music or a sound effect**. Audio can be a very striking start to a presentation. Music can set the mood or tone or convey a message. It's particularly useful to pump energy into a room or calm a room down, perhaps after an activity or break.

  Sound effects can also transport people very quickly into a certain mindset or location. One of my keynote speeches is about the concept of 'engagement' (how all communications should be a two-way process) and opens with a blank slide that has a looped clip of the engaged tone from a phone on it. I click so it plays before I walk on and it immediately sets the audience wondering what I'm going to talk about.

  I've also heard sounds including aircraft flying over, rainfall or the sound of a crowd cheering used to open presentations.

- A final idea for a strong opening is to **preview the end of your presentation**:

  ○ 'If I told you that in 15 minutes I'm going to change the way you use sales figures – for ever – would you believe me?'

  ○ 'By the time I've finished this presentation in 45 minutes time you're going to know how big this year's bonus is going to be.'

  ○ 'In the next 10 minutes I'm going to give you three ways to grow your business.'

All these also set up the opportunity to revisit this opening statement at the end of your presentation – but more on ending or closing your presentation in a couple of chapters time.

This list of ideas is in no way exhaustive. Think about how you can really make an impact with your opening. It's an opportunity to be creative and lift your presentation above the mundane and 'same old, same old' to grab your audience's attention.

Just as I explained when talking about humour, your opening must be sensitive to the tone you need to set, the content you're presenting and the context in which you're presenting. *But*, don't feel that doing something creative and a bit different will somehow undermine your credibility and professionalism. You don't have to be boring to be professional – in fact the opposite is true. Audiences respect presenters who go out of their way to do something different and something engaging. You're making an audience feel they're *worth* doing something creative for.

One final tip on the opening of your presentation: know your first words off by heart. I'm not a big fan of learning and delivering a script parrot-fashion, but you *must* learn and be able to deliver your opening line – just the first couple of sentences – with confidence. Get those right and the rest of the presentation will feel so much easier. Fluff them and it immediately suggests to your audience that you're nervous and that you don't know your stuff. Not the way you want to open your presentation.

Exercise

Thinking about the presentation you set objectives for in a previous chapter, what technique will you use to give it a really memorable, impactful and effective opening?

If you don't know what you want to achieve in your presentation, your audience never will.

Harvey Diamond

Structuring that tricky bit in the middle

As I said in an earlier chapter, not only does your presentation as a whole need a distinct structure, the important central section of content (normally the longest of the three sections) needs its own structure. This will make it easier for your audience to follow and easier to understand, thus making it more effective. It will also make it easier for you to remember and deliver. So a win-win for you and the audience.

There are a number of ways you can structure the content of your presentation.

Past, present, future

One of the most common and probably one of the easiest to use structures is past, present, future. Look at the topic you need to cover and split your content into where we were (past), where we are (present) and where we're going/where we want to be (future).

Most stories follow this chronological structure (although sometimes 'past' is told as 'backstory' once the story has started) and we're used to following a thread along a timeline. Try not to jump around in time (leave that to Dr Who), but talk through your topic from beginning to expected or desired end.

For example, if you have to deliver sales figures and talk about targets, you could start talking about where the business was this time last year or last month (past), the current situation and figures (present) and then the targets you need to meet (future).

You don't have to give equal weight to each section of your presentation – it might be that you look briefly at the past to give some context, then move on to look at the present situation in some depth before just glancing ahead into the future.

Three main points and the fishbone template

It's generally accepted that most people will struggle to remember more than three main points from your presentation. Our friend Aristotle pointed this out when he talked about the importance of making your point by delivering your message as a list of three things.

If you don't believe this, try it. A few days after you've given a presentation try surveying a few people who were in the audience. Most will struggle (unless really pushed) to remember more than three things you said, and they may well not be the three things you wanted or expected them to remember. I have a couple of quite dramatic personal stories I used to tell as part of my presentations, but now rarely tell them as I became aware that people were remembering those stories rather than the content and message they were meant to be illustrating.

The three things that people *do* remember can be revealing too, as they're often either three incredibly detailed things that clearly resonated with that person, or three very broad topics, which may reflect how you presented the information. We're remarkably well trained to look for lists of three points and if they're clear and well presented you'll find people will write them down, which is always a good sign.

The starting point for using this structure is to ask yourself: 'If my audience remember three things from this presentation – what do I want them to be?' and then you build your presentation around them, splitting your content into three main sections to reflect them.

The fishbone template

The fishbone template is a more advanced structure for your middle section, although it also gives you space to structure your opening and closing sections, too. At its heart are the three main points you want your audience to remember.

Figure 1 shows the fishbone template and maps out how you can structure your presentation around your three main points.

Figure 1 Structuring your presentation: the fishbone template

Opening: image, video, questions, etc.

Introduce yourself and your topic

Purpose or aim: why we're here

Main point 1
Summary: Why is this point important or relevant?

Stories
Evidence
Support matter
Arguments
Explanation
Research
Case studies

Signpost to next section

Main point 2
Summary: Why is this point important or relevant?

Stories
Evidence
Support matter
Arguments
Explanation
Research
Case studies

Signpost to next section

Main point 3
Summary: Why is this point important or relevant?

Stories
Evidence
Support matter
Arguments
Explanation
Research
Case studies

Signpost to next section

Recap or summary of main points

Call to action and next steps

Final impression: image, video etc.

Figure 2 Structuring your presentation: the fishbone template (blank)

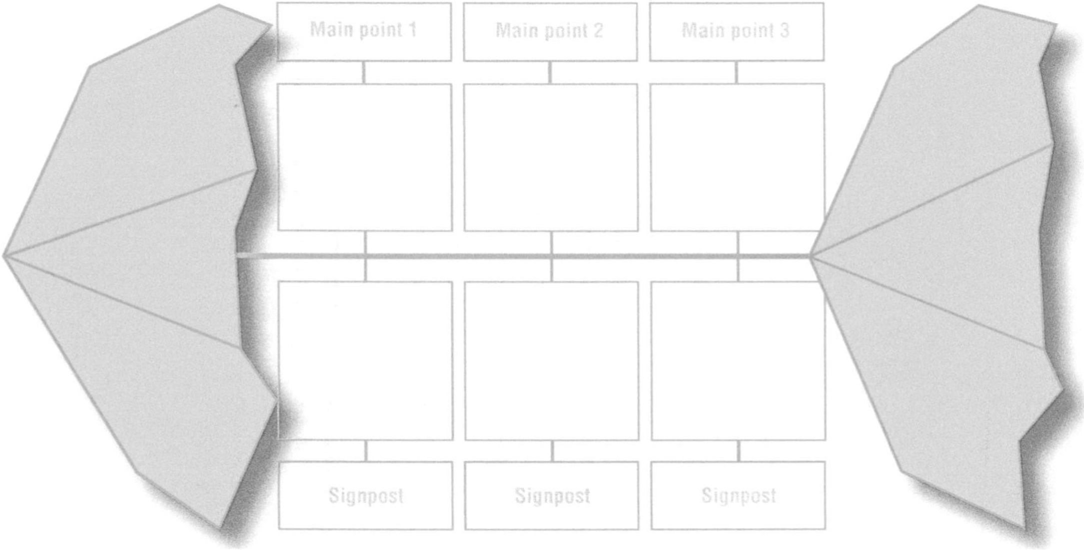

Main point 3

Main point 2

Main point 1

Signpost

Signpost

Signpost

It works left to right, head to tail. Your opening section, as discussed in the previous chapter, fits in the head and includes your opening; introducing yourself and your topic; and perhaps outlining your purpose or aim for the presentation and laying out the three main points you're about to make.

You then move into your content by starting with main point 1. You need to outline this point clearly and in a very obvious way. Put it as a headline on a slide accompanied by a strong image that illustrates it. Say it out loud, more than once (repetition is a great way to help people remember it). Ask people what they know about this topic or point, to get them thinking about it.

You then go on to explain why this main point is important and relevant, not only to the overall topic, but also to the audience. This point might be important because:

- if we don't all take this on board, we'll miss our target
- if we don't sort this problem out, we won't succeed
- this is one of our organisation's key values
- this is one of our new products we're about to launch.

Once you've summarised why this point is important, you then provide evidence for its importance and go into more detail. In this section you might include a case study or example, some research or statistics, a testimonial, your arguments or an explanation. All this evidence should serve to back up and illustrate the main point.

When you've finished this main point you need to make it obvious that you're moving on by signposting.

Signposting your way through your presentation

Signposting is letting your audience know that you're finishing one of your three main points, so mentally they're able to file that away in the 'to remember' part of their brain and clear the decks for the next main point that's about to come their way.

You can signpost in a number of ways. You can signpost verbally:

- 'So, that was my first point. Now I'm going to move on to my second point…'
- 'That's all I have to say on that topic. Before we move on does anyone have any questions?'

You can also signpost visually that you're moving on:

- Repeat the 'headline' slide you used to introduce the topic. This helps to signal that you've come full circle.
- Move to a blank slide and use one of the verbal cues above.
- Turn over the paper you've just used on a flip chart or wipe clean the whiteboard to show that that information is now no longer needed and you're moving on to the next point.
- Move from one position in the room or on the stage to another, again using a verbal cue at the same time.

If you don't use visual or verbal signposting cues to signal you're about to move on, your audience will very quickly lose track of where you are. If they're not sure where you are or whether you've moved on yet, they'll soon lose interest.

Once you've made it clear that point 1 is finished then you can signpost that you're moving to point 2. You then work through exactly the same process, discussing why this point is important and illustrating it with evidence, then signposting and moving on to point 3.

Once you've worked through all three main points (which could be five minutes per point or an hour per point in a training course type of presentation) you then move on to your conclusion and closing, which we'll discuss in the next chapter.

If you want to try the fishbone template to structure your presentations, you can download the blank template and an explainer from bit.ly/2ctuGrn

The non-linear approach – let your audience set the structure

This is a structure that is probably best tried once you're a fairly confident presenter.

You break down your presentation content into bite-sized topic 'nuggets' and then let your audience decide the order in which they want to hear those nuggets of content.

Start with a strong opening that sets up your topic, outlines your themes and lists what the audience will be able to take from your presentation. Then reveal the topic nuggets the audience can choose from and invite them to make their first choice.

There are three ways to do this:

1. Have a slide on the screen listing all the nuggets – if you're confident with slides, you can animate the slide so a nugget disappears once you've covered it. Figure 3 shows an

example used by one of the UK's top speakers and CEO experts, Roger Harrop.

Figure 3 Slide by speaker Roger Harrop when using a non-linear presentation structure. The audience choose the topic they want to hear about next

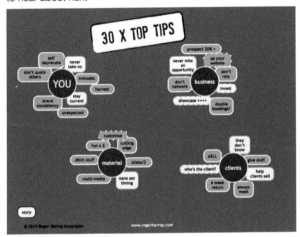

2 I tend to use a deck of cue cards with a word or phrase on one side. I spread them out and offer them to a member of the audience and ask them to pick a card, a bit like a magician might ask you to pick a playing card. I ask the audience member to read out the word or phrase on the card and then I talk about that topic nugget. I can use the reverse of the card for a couple of bullet points to act as a reminder of what I want to say on that particular topic (Figure 4).

Figure 4 Cue cards used by the author when delivering a non-linear presentation. An audience member picks a card to decide on the next topic. The bullet points on the reverse are an aide-memoire for the author

③ In a similar vein you can put anything from slips of paper to ping pong balls in a hat, bag or box and ask people to pull one out, each triggering the next nugget.

This can be a very engaging and interactive way to present your topic, with the audience feeling they're dictating the content (although of course it's your usual content, just delivered in a slightly random order). The downside of this is that you can't control the order, so each nugget has to be stand-alone and can't depend on you having delivered a certain other nugget first in order to be understandable.

You also need to be keenly aware of your timings and how long you spend on each nugget; if you don't have time to get through all of them, you can leave your audience feeling short-changed if they've missed out on certain parts of your content.

As I suggested earlier, this is perhaps not a structure to use for your first-ever presentation, but it can be a good way to challenge yourself if you're delivering the same content regularly. It's also a great way to keep it fresh for your audience, especially if you're presenting to them regularly, such as at a weekly or monthly team meeting.

Exercise

Continuing to work on the presentation you were thinking about in the last exercise. What structure are you going to use for the content of your presentation? Why do you think that is the best structure to use?

The success of your presentation will be
judged not by the knowledge you send but
by what the listener receives.

Lilly Walters

Close on a high note

Once you've delivered all your content, you need to round up your presentation with the third and final part of your overall structure – your closing.

There are some classic terrible endings to a presentation, such as the shrug of the shoulders and a muttered 'that's it', or clicking past your last slide so suddenly the audience is looking at your computer desktop or your PowerPoint workspace.

Or just

Stopping.

A strong closing section is important for several reasons:

- It's your chance to reinforce your key messages or points with a swift recap.
- It's also your opportunity to tell people what you want them to do with what you've just told them, to issue a call to action.
- Your close is the final impression you'll leave with an audience. Do you want that final impression to be good or bad?

Your closing section happens when you finish your content, but before you open the floor for questions. Don't add anything new that hasn't appeared earlier in your presentation as your closing section or conclusion is about recapping and reinforcing what you've already said. This is the final part in Aristotle's 'tell them what you're going to tell them, tell it to them, then tell them what you've just told them' rule.

If you do nothing else, make it clear this is the end and don't just peter out, especially if you want to generate a round of applause or a vote of thanks at the end.

Some ideas for a strong closing section:

- **A summary**. Always include a summary of your main points, especially if you've used the three main points structure or fishbone template outlined in the last chapter.

- **Call to action**. You *must* include a call to action. What do you want people to go away and actually do with all the information you've just given them? Do you want them to go back to their desks and do something differently? Do you want them to change their lives? Do you want them to visit a website, book a ticket, cascade the information or buy your book?

  If there isn't a call to action to be given, what was the point of giving the presentation? Have you just wasted everyone's time if there's nothing for people to do next? Make your call to action explicit, and spell it out on a slide if necessary. Don't expect your audience to extrapolate what you want them to do from all the information you've just given them. Make it clear and easy to understand so there's no room for misunderstanding.

- **Image, video or sound effect**. Just as in your opening section, an image, video or sound clip can make a very effective close. You can use the same image you started with, which gives a great sense of closure, or you can use an image that has changed in some way. A popular example is opening with an image of diverging pathways or roads, sending the message that we have to make a decision about which way to go or that we lack direction. You would then close with the same image, but now there is a signpost showing the way or someone heading confidently down a particular path.

- **A quote**. Leave your audience with a 'final thought', perhaps a pertinent quote from a great thinker, delivered verbally or on a slide.

- **Revisit the opening**. You can revisit your opening section, especially if you opened by previewing the end. 'Do you remember that I said 30 minutes ago that I was going to tell you how we could all meet our targets? Do you all now understand how we're going to do that?'

- **A quiz**. A quiz can be a fun way to recap your main points and also check that your audience have understood and remembered what you've said. Offer a small prize (chocolate or wine seem to do the trick) to the first person that can correctly answer perhaps three questions about what you said.

- **Something funny**. Humour is also just as good as a close as it is as an opener. Sending your audience out with a smile or a laugh means they leave with a very positive impression. As before, don't feel you need a gag – find a vaguely topic-related cartoon or video to use as your final slide.

Exercise

Sticking with the presentation you were working on in previous chapters, how can you bring it to a memorable, impactful and effective close?

If you have an important point to make, don't try to be subtle or clever. Use a pile driver. Hit the point once. Then come back and hit it again. Then hit it a third time – a tremendous whack.

Winston S. Churchill

Using slides during your presentation

Once you've got your content created and structured, you need to consider how you're going to bring that content and your message to life for your audience.

You could, of course, stand in front of your audience, read your script (or even worse, read your slides), drone at them, not make eye contact and send them to sleep or scurrying for the door. Please don't.

Why do we need to 'bring it to life'?

Remember when we looked at your audience's likely objectives? I mentioned the fact that one of the top – if not *the* top – objective for most audience members is to not be bored by your presentation.

You want to make your presentation:

- Memorable – for the right reasons
- Enjoyable (or, at the very least, interesting)
- Easy to understand
- Effective

This is why it's so important to bring it to life, to make it engaging. A dull presentation is boring to watch and listen to so your audience will quickly switch off. No one meets their objectives in a dull presentation. There are lots of ways of making your presentation interesting and engaging, which we'll explore in more detail in the next chapter, but let's start with the tool most people turn to first.

Slides

Yes, the dreaded/lauded/loved/hated slides – usually created in and often referred to simply as PowerPoint. Actually PowerPoint is a pretty cool tool in the right hands, but used badly (or, dare I say it, lazily) it's the death knell for an engaging presentation.

I'm going to use the word 'slide' rather than referring to 'PowerPoint' because, as we shall discover, there are plenty of other tools to use to create visual aids to project on a screen – and that's what a slide is, a visual aid on a screen.

Some people find it inconceivable that you can give or watch a presentation without slides. I've had people turn up to presentation coaching sessions to give a 60 second introductory presentation – with their slides on a USB stick. If you can't present for 60 seconds without slides, there's a problem. Hint: it's not the slides that are the problem.

I've had people book me to give a presentation only to express shock and worry when they ask for my slides in advance and I say that there aren't any. One booker just wailed, 'So what are they going to look at?' I pointed out that I may not have the looks of George Clooney, but I've yet to have anyone drop dead from being forced to look at me for 30 minutes. On the day, a number of delegates complimented me on the fact I didn't use slides.

Slides can be the most amazing boon to a presentation and I'm assuming that you probably will want to use slides at some point – I use them from time to time when I think they'll serve a particular purpose. Just be aware that they're not a prerequisite for giving a presentation and we'll explore some of the alternatives to slides in the next chapter.

What's the point of slides?

> **Top tip**
>
> The slides are there *for your audience*. They are there to bring your content to life, to make it easier to understand and easier to remember.

Let's get one classic error out the way up front:

> **Top tip**
>
> The slides are *not* your script.

They are not there to guide you through your presentation. You must not be reliant on your slides in order to deliver your presentation. There are two very good reasons why you mustn't be reliant on your slides:

1. If you are reliant on your slides to guide you through and act as your script or prompts, there is a very strong probability that you will stop looking at your audience and look at your slides instead. It doesn't matter whether they're on a laptop in front of you or the screen behind you, you'll lose eye contact with the very people you're talking to. In the worst case, you'll end up with your back to the audience, reading your slides word for word. I've seen it happen many times – and I'm sure you have too.

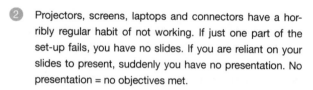 Projectors, screens, laptops and connectors have a horribly regular habit of not working. If just one part of the set-up fails, you have no slides. If you are reliant on your slides to present, suddenly you have no presentation. No presentation = no objectives met.

Creating slides

PowerPoint is a powerful tool when you know what you're doing with it. But I think it has 'feature bloat' that makes it less than ideal to use, and many of the templates and design features are looking dated and encourage boring slides. Here are some alternative tools I think you should explore and use.

● Keynote (www.apple.com/uk/mac/keynote). If you're an Apple user, make sure you're using this in preference to PowerPoint. It's easier to get to grips with (it behaves like most other Apple apps so feels more familiar than the Microsoft equivalent), and with much more modern templates and styling it creates far more visually appealing slides. The iPad version is less fully featured, but still easy and effective to use.

● Prezi (https://prezi.com/). Slide decks can be created with the feel of an animated film, sweeping from slide to slide, zooming in and out to the slides, showing graphical representations of the whole presentation. It helps to get you away from strictly linear presentations, as you design on a 'canvas' rather than in a sequence. Prezi can create beautiful, fluid presentations that really do bring the content to life. Used badly, however, a Prezi presentation can make an audience feel seasick as the screen swoops and whirls, and the animations can look a little tricksy. It has a steep learning curve, too, but those who spend the time to do it well can produce excellent slides. Be aware that your slides will be stored online and are searchable if you don't take a paid subscription.

- Haiku Deck (www.haikudeck.com). I love Haiku Deck. In my experience it's virtually impossible to create a boring slide with this simple-to-use online tool. The defining feature is the use of full-screen images with minimal text. You start with a slide that allows a maximum of two lines of text – perhaps a headline and subtitle, or even just one word. Once you've entered your text, Haiku Deck will suggest a gallery of relevant images, culled from photo sharing site Flickr. Cleverly, it will only suggest images that are covered by Creative Commons licenses, so are free to use. Figure 5 is an example I made in literally 30 seconds, and I had 30+ images to choose from.

Figure 5 An example of a slide created using Haiku Deck

The images vary in quality (some are professional stock shots, others amateur snapshots), but you can also import your own images, logos and so on. There is also an option to create really simple but stylish graphs, charts, and so forth using your own data, and you can also add YouTube videos and presenter notes. You can present direct from Haiku Deck (make sure you'll have decent Wi-Fi) or export to PDF or a PowerPoint file.

It's very easy to learn to use and then very quick to produce excellent slide decks. Check out www.haikudeck.com or their app for iPad and Android, which is probably even nicer than their web version. This is my tool of choice on those occasions when I do want to use slides.

- There are lots more tools and it's worth experimenting and exploring to find the one that suits you and the presentations you want to give. Powtoon (www.powtoon.com) creates animated videos and presentations with a cartoon feel. Canva (www.canva.com) has some beautiful slide templates and uses great images. Phonto (www.phon.to) is a mobile app that's useful for adding words to images. WordSwag (www.wordswag.co) is another great app for adding text to your photos, with some beautiful fonts and templates for a very professional, designer look.

Top tip

If I've got time before a presentation, I'll take a photo of the audience coming in or even outside having coffee, use Phonto to add a few words of welcome, mentioning the client or event name, then drop this into my Keynote or Haiku Deck presentation as an opening slide. Audiences love seeing themselves on screen and the client or booker appreciates the personalisation.

One of the advantages of using these tools is that your presentations really stand out from the morass of identikit presentations, just by looking different. Don't feel you have to redesign your slide deck from scratch in one go, either. Just dropping in some more creative slides made using tools such as these will really help lift your existing presentation.

So what does a great slide look like?

Top tip

When creating a slide, your aims are to engage your audience, to add impact and to aid understanding.

In his book *PowerPoint Surgery* (2013), which I highly recommend, slide expert Lee Jackson likens a slide to a billboard. When you drive past a billboard it has one or two seconds to make an impact and communicate its message – and a slide should do the same.

Top tip

The key adage for slides is 'less is more'.

The biggest problem with slides is that people try to cram far too much information on each slide. When you start designing a slide (and try to think of slide creation as 'designing' rather than just 'writing') ask yourself: What's the one thing I want the audience to take away from this slide? Is there one fact, one figure, one idea – or one mood or tone that you'd like them to experience or remember? Then concentrate on that one thing and remove everything else. To my mind it's better to have 20 slides with one idea or figure on each than 10 slides crammed with information – you just move through those 20 faster, which makes your presentation feel pacier, too.

The best and most effective slides often have no words at all. In fact a well-chosen image can express more than words and it's a far more engaging way of making a point.

For example, which of Figure 6 or Figure 7 makes for a more interesting, engaging slide?

Figure 6 A rather dull approach to a standard slide

Figure 7 A much more modern, stylish approach to a slide that fulfils the same purpose as the slide featured in Figure 6

Top tip

When using images, use them at full size, allowing the image to 'bleed' off the edge of the slide, as this gives a very clean, modern style that looks great on a big screen, such as in Figure 7.

Sometimes you might want to add one or two words to an image, just to reinforce your message. By offsetting an image such as Figure 7, you can create 'blank' space for a few words, as in Figure 8.

Figure 8 Use white space on slides to place a small amount of pertinent text

Top tip

Don't be scared of blank space on a slide and don't be afraid to keep it simple. Sometimes you can make the most impact by keeping it as simple as possible, as shown in Figure 9.

Figure 9 Keeping it simple on a slide can have the greatest impact

Results

If you're going to use images on your slides (and you really should), try to avoid relying on stock shots for your illustrations because:

- they're often very clichéd images – the handshake, the meeting in progress, the 'head in hands' worried boss...

- they're available to everyone and used by a lot of people so they make every presentation look the same

- a lot of these images are used illegally, cribbed from Google Image, but photo agencies are now using sophisticated tools to track use of their images and are invoicing offenders for thousands of pounds or dollars

- they're really dull and indicate a lazy approach to a presentation.

Look for surprising or original images – or take your own. I commissioned a photographer to take a set of images for me that illustrated different aspects of my work and the topics I speak and train on, to use on my website and as slides.

For example, the 'microphone' image in Figure 7 was actually shot to illustrate my media training work, but in fact works very well as a slide, too. It means I have ownership of the image – you won't (or at least shouldn't) see it used by any other presenter.

Exercise

What sort of images could you use to represent the topics you need to present on? Make a list of six images that would be really pertinent and effective. Could you take them yourself or engage a photographer or designer to create them for you?

Death by bullet point

I've no idea who first came up with the 666 rule of bullet points (Figure 10) and my research hasn't thrown up any answers, so if it was you, 'thank you' as you've saved us all from even more boring presentations.

Figure 10 Death by bullet point

- Have you ever produced slides like this?

- Dull, aren't they? Visually uninteresting and horribly repetitive, they force the audience to read along with you…

- …and quite often read ahead of you so they get to the end before you and are drumming their fingers waiting for you to catch up.

- If you must use bullet points, remember the 666 rule of PowerPoint:

  - No more than 6 bullet points per page

  - No more than 6 words per bullet point

  - No more than 6 minutes per slide

Top tip

Remember: 'less is more' and abide by the 666 rule when using bullet points.

More than six bullets per page will make it overcrowded if you want to keep the font size readable. A bullet point should be a maximum of six words, ideally just one or two; if it's a full sentence, you'll end up reading it, as will your audience. If your slide of bullets is on screen for more than six minutes your audience will have read it, got bored and switched off.

The other saying you regularly hear applied to the use of bullet points is that 'bullets kill people – don't let bullets kill your presentation'. I really do believe that if you start to create a slide with a bullet point, you're about to create a boring slide – and is that really what you want to do? Occasionally a bullet point slide can be useful, especially in a more training-oriented presentation, outlining, say, the five key points or the four core values, but use them judiciously as slide after slide of bullet after bullet gets dull very fast and you'll see eyes glaze over.

Top tip

If you must use bullet points, split them up across your presentation, never having two or more slides of bullet points back to back.

The other, much better, option is to disguise your bullet points to keep them interested (Figure 11).

Figure 11 A more visually interesting approach to using bullet points

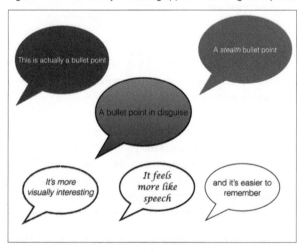

Figure 11 conforms to the 666 rule and (although I'm no designer) is considerably more interesting than a row of dots down the left side of the slide. Look for some suitable clip art and use that to break up your bullet points and make them more engaging.

Oh, and whizzing in your bullet points from screen left, or having them appear in a burst of flame or drop from the sky doesn't help, as your audience is distracted from the content by the improbable behaviour of the bullet point.

> **Top tip**
>
> Resist the temptation to use every animation trick that PowerPoint offers, as your presentation ends up looking gimmicky and as if you're trying to deflect attention from the dull delivery.

Bullet points can work very well in documents and on handouts (and in books like this, for that matter), breaking down blocks of text into manageable bite-sized chunks. On a slide, they just get very dull, very quickly. You have been warned...

A few other do's and don'ts, hints and tips for using slides

- Invest in a 'clicker' to control your slides without having to return to your laptop every time you're ready to move on. They retail from around £20 and are worth the investment.

- Know what screen ratio of the display or projector you'll be working with. Some are the almost square 4:3 while others are the widescreen 16:9. PowerPoint and Keynote both allow you to adjust your slides to either setting, but you can suddenly find your images distorted and your slide design ruined. It's far easier to create them in the right ratio in the first place.

- Corporate slide templates are pretty much an anathema to building an engaging slide deck. They're restrictive, old-fashioned and unnecessary. By all means use your organisation's logo on the first and last slides and possibly even on the structural headline slides throughout, but your audience know where you're from so give them the best possible slides, not a brand overload. Corporate template slide + bullet points = immediate audience switch off.

- In a similar vein, you don't need to put your contact details on every slide. No one is suddenly going to want to call or email you when they see slide 22, half way through your presentation. Put them on the slide that appears during and after the questions and answers (Q&A) session at the end.

  The one exception to this is your Twitter username. You may want people to tweet about you and your content during your presentation and they may need reminding of your username to tag. Again, don't put it on every slide as it will make your slides look cluttered and ruin any full-screen images. Put it on specific slides that you'd like your audience to tweet about.

- Make use of blank slides to create pauses in your presentation. If there is something on the screen, the audience will look at it rather than you. As discussed when we looked at bullet points, if something is there too long the audience will just switch off. A blank slide brings their focus back to you and gives you a chance to talk without distraction.

Top tip

It's worth remembering that when you're in Slide Show mode in PowerPoint or Keynote, pressing the 'B' key on your keyboard will turn the screen black or the 'W' key will turn it white. Press any key and it immediately returns to what it was showing. This is a useful way to clear the screen if you haven't got a blank slide in your deck.

- If you have video embedded into your slides make sure you've had a technical run-through first, especially if you've had to transfer your presentation onto someone else's computer. (I now insist on presenting from my own laptop unless there really is no other way.) Set the video to 'play on click' so it plays when you're ready and doesn't autostart when it appears on screen. Check the audio, too, as you may need to let the audiovisual (AV) person know that they'll need the volume turned up.

- Don't fall into the trap of creating what designer and author Garr Reynolds calls 'Slideuments'. In his excellent book, *Presentation Zen* (2011), Reynolds discusses how we often try to make our slides serve two purposes – as a slide in a presentation, but also as a document that can be printed, distributed and understood even by people who weren't at the presentation. The end result is that the slides don't fulfil either role properly.

  Create your slides, then create a separate document (not necessarily based on those slides) for distribution to audience members either on paper or electronically. If someone who wasn't at your presentation can read your slides afterwards (whether printed or as a PDF) and fully understand the message and takeaways of the presentation, then perhaps you, the presenter, were superfluous? Why waste everyone's time with a presentation when you could have just given them something to read instead?

Top tip

Slides are for use on screen during a presentation. A document is a completely difference medium. Just as you wouldn't put a Word document on a slide (you wouldn't, would you?), don't try to turn a slide into a document. Just because you *can* print slides doesn't mean you should.

Exercise

If you use slides, how are you going to update, redesign, amend and otherwise change them to create a modern, effective slide deck? What tools are you going to use? What images? How few words can you get away with? Do you need slides at all?

Embracing a world without slides

As we discussed in the last chapter, you don't need slides in order to give a presentation. In fact there are some definite benefits to not using slides.

If you're presenting as part of a long meeting or conference and everyone else is using slides, *not* using them will make your presentation stand out from the crowd.

Not using slides also shows confidence, not only in your ability to engage and hold an audience, but also in your knowledge and expertise.

The other problem with slides is that they are linear, that is, you're stuck with them in that order. Not using slides allows you to move around in your material, adding or dropping elements to respond to feedback from the room. Audiences hate seeing a presenter flick past slides due to lack of time or preparation. All that says to the audience is that there is valuable content that they're missing out on.

Scripts and prompts

If you'd like to embrace presenting without slides, but rely on them to prompt yourself through your presentation, there are other options. You could try learning the whole thing by heart so you can deliver it from memory, but to be honest I don't recommend it. Quite apart from the fact that learning a 30 minute presentation word for word is really hard work, it does also tend to mean you stay 'in your head' rather than 'in the room' while you're speaking.

You can often tell if someone is delivering a learned script because they end up using a slightly odd sing-song delivery as they 'recite' what they want to say. They also tend to have little or no interaction with the audience, because if they lose their place in their script in order to answer a question, for example, they've then got to remember where they left off.

Top tip

My strong advice is to know what you want to say, but don't know your words.

By that I mean that you have a careful plan and structure for what you want to cover, but don't write it longhand or learn it. Instead, know the order your points come in and talk about them as you get to them. Don't forget, you know this content already, you're just talking about it, seemingly 'off the cuff'.

If I do want prompts of some sort, I usually use cue cards or white postcards with bullet points on them. I hold them discreetly in my hand (or sometimes leave them on a table near where I'm presenting) so I can just glance at them if I can't remember where I need to go next in my talk.

More tips on scripts and prompts

- Never have your prompt notes on a piece of paper. First because, if you're nervous, that piece of paper will betray any shake in your hand, and second because a piece of paper (or a sheaf of papers) looks scrappy and will often end up being folded or scrunched up where you took it out of your pocket.

- Never go on stage with a script written out longhand, word for word. This is because you will end up reading it, meaning you're looking at your script and not making eye contact with your audience. This also increases the chances of you speaking in a monotone. If you do glance up from reading it, to look at your audience, when you glance back down you'll probably have lost your place, leaving you flustered and looking unprofessional.

Bringing your presentation to life without slides

I nearly called this section 'the low-tech solutions', but that suggests that alternatives to slides are somehow second best or less impressive, when nothing could be further from the truth. Some of these ideas and tools can be far more effective than even the best designed slides.

Flip charts and whiteboards

Don't overlook the humble flip chart. Most meeting rooms or conference venues will have a flip chart stand somewhere to hand and they can make great visual aids for presentations, although in a larger room you do need to make sure everyone can see it.

The beauty of flip charts is that you can generate visual aids and engaging visual content *live*.

> **Top tip**
>
> An audience is more likely to remember something they've seen you write or draw right in front of them, than if the same graphic had just appeared on a screen in front of them.

Just the fact that the information appears slowly as pen crosses paper means they can follow along and will remember it more easily.

This is particularly true if your presentation contains a lot of graphs or figures on slides. If you've presented more than three or four such slides on the trot, especially if they're quite similar, the audience will stop differentiating between them.

> **Top tip**
>
> Rather than show yet another graph, blank the screen, move to the flip chart and draw this graph live in front of the audience.

This is your expertise and knowledge on display right in front of them. This is particularly good if you want to show a trend over time rather than a specific figure.

> **Top tip**
>
> If you are planning to use a flip chart, prepare some flip chart paper in advance with some notes for yourself in light pencil along one edge. They are invisible to your audience, but prompt you to include all the pertinent information or figures. Don't, however, pre-draw all your charts or graphs, as you lose the live creation element and may as well just put them on slides.

If there isn't a flip chart present, you might find there's a white-board, which serves exactly the same purpose, or you can buy A1 sized 'sheets' of whiteboard-like paper that can be stuck to any wall, a bit like a giant write-on/wipe-off Post-it™ note.

A flip chart or whiteboard is also a good place to collect audi-ence input – perhaps noting questions as they come up so you can address them at the end of your presentation, or bringing together your audience's ideas or suggestions.

> **Top tip**
>
> Audiences like to see that their input is valued, not just acknowledged or, even worse, ignored. This really helps them to feel included, so record it by making a public note of it on a flip chart or whiteboard.

Don't forget that turning over the page on a flip chart or wiping clean the whiteboard is also a good way to signpost that you're moving on to a new section or topic in your presentation.

Props

The term 'prop' always makes me think of a table of miscella-neous items backstage in a theatre, waiting to be taken on stage by an actor to be used in the action. Without that prop the story couldn't be told. The same is true of your presentation.

> **Top tip**
>
> Show, don't tell. Are there physical items that will help you tell your story and help your audience understand what you're saying more clearly and easily?

You can use all sorts of things as props, but here are just a few suggestions.

- **Product**. If you're selling or promoting something, let the audience, see, feel, touch, experience it. It's remarkable the number of times I've seen people try to present or pitch a product (and even bid for investment in a product) without actually bringing any samples of the product in question along with them.

- **Tools**. If you're presenting a service, bring along the tools you use, whether physical tools or digital tools. Let us see how you provide that service. Let us see the results and how they are generated.

- **Virtual props**. Audiences are used to being online on their phones or tablets during a presentation (to be on social media if nothing else) so you can take advantage of that fact and rather than just showing them a website or app on a big screen, get them to experience it themselves. For smaller presentations (such as pitch meetings) take along preloaded iPads that will help you demonstrate.

- **Books**. They might feel low-tech after iPads, but don't underestimate people's engagement and pleasure at being introduced to a book they might enjoy and/or find useful.

- **Build something live**. Use a prop such as LEGO bricks to build something live in front of your audience (although bear in mind the size of the room). Build a giant bar chart or construct a model of your new product using LEGO or a similar construction toy. In the same way that audiences will remember graphs they've watched being drawn in front of them, so they'll remember the creation of something three dimensional.

Figure 12 Bar charts with a difference: Jelly Babies and LEGO used to illustrate figures in a presentation.

- **Food**. People like cake. Or sweets. Or drinks. Apart from it feeling like they're getting something tasty for free, food or drink can be very effectively used to make a point. I've seen jelly babies used at a high-powered board meeting to illustrate the breakdown of staff contracts, with different coloured jelly babies representing different sections of the workforce. Of course, as soon as the presentation was over, the board then devoured the jelly workforce, which was a bit startling. I've also seen beer being poured into different sized containers to illustrate a presentation about electoral reform. Both those presentations stick in my head because I saw the message created and represented in front of me. And because I like jelly babies and beer.

- **Handouts can be handy**. While they can seem low-tech, handouts of various types can also be a great way to bring a presentation to life. If you have got detailed information to impart, such as a cash flow forecast or a complex organisational structure diagram, putting it into your audience's hands means they can look at it in detail rather than squinting at lots of small figures or text on a slide. They can also annotate it with their own notes, then take that back to their desk to refer to later.

Top tip

Handouts, whether they are a sheet of paper, a booklet or even a book, are a good way to put your contact details into your audience's hands. This is especially important if you're selling, pitching or asking them to contact you after your presentation.

Exercise

What props could you use in your next presentation to help bring it to life?

Engagement

Engagement is about making your presentation a two-way process or conversation with your audience. More and more event organisers, meeting planners and speaker bookers are asking how presenters will encourage engagement and interactivity with their audience during their speeches. The days of 'stand and deliver' speech-type presentations seem to be waning.

There are numerous ways you can encourage engagement during your presentation.

- **Discussion**. Ask your audience members to turn to the person next to them/behind them/across the table from them and discuss a point you have just made. This enables them to explore that point in their own words and gets them thinking about their own response to it. Two tips: first, rather than just saying 'discuss this', pose a question such as: 'How would this affect your business?' Second, have a bell, whistle or some other way to draw the audience discussion to a close in order to bring their attention back to you. It's slightly more professional than shouting 'Oi' or wolf-whistling to attract their attention!

- **Votes and straw polls**. Ask your audience what they think about something. Ask for a show of hands, to cheer for their preferred option or even to form a line across a room to indicate their strength of feeling on an issue, from 'completely agree' to 'completely disagree' at either end. It can be fascinating to repeat a vote at the beginning and end of your presentation, to see whether anything has changed.

- **Social media**. If there is no hashtag set for the event you're speaking at, announce one for your presentation and encourage people to tweet their comments or questions – then at the end of your presentation have a look at Twitter on your phone or tablet to read out audience comments and answer their questions.

- **Apps**. There are plenty of apps now available to allow your audience to engage with your presentation, from downloading and interacting with your slides to taking part in opinion polls, the results of which can be shown live on screen. Check out Glisser (www.glisser.com) or a very cool app called CrowdMics (www.crowdmics.com) that turns audience members' phones into microphones that can be picked up by the sound system, so you don't have to worry about getting a roving mic to someone in order to hear their question.

- **Q&A**. Probably the oldest, simplest and often most effective form of audience engagement is the Q&A session. You should let an audience know at the beginning of your presentation when they can ask questions: at certain points, at the end or whether you are happy to take questions all the way through. If you're not sure your presentation is really engaging your audience (perhaps you've misjudged the existing level of knowledge or skill in the room), then scrapping your prepared content and straight going into a Q&A format means the audience can dictate what you talk about, making it far more likely that they'll get what they need from your session.

Exercise

Is your presentation currently just a one-way process? How are you going to make your presentation a two-way process and get your audience members actively involved and engaged?

Mix it up to bring it to life

Often the best way to bring your presentation to life is to mix up all these methods and tools. By including some slides (you could use them for a part of your presentation rather than the whole thing), some props, some flip chart work and a mix of engagement methods, your audience are fully involved and don't have the inclination or opportunity to switch off and ignore what you're saying.

Good presenters don't just stand and talk at their audience. They set out to bring it to life to ensure both they and their audience meet their objectives and leave the presentation feeling it was a really valuable use of their time.

Presenting figures, numbers and data

'It's all very well being creative with your presentation when you're presenting something creative,' is a regular cry I hear, 'but I only present figures, so I have to use lots of charts, graphs and spreadsheets. How do I bring my presentations to life?'

Presenting data or lots of figures can be tricky, there's no doubt about it. As soon as a graph or a screenshot of a spreadsheet goes up on a slide, half your audience switches off. Data doesn't have to be dull, however. Figures can be fun – but it's up to you to ensure they are.

The problem is that if an audience member isn't used to looking at numbers or interpreting spreadsheets, it can be very hard for them to extrapolate what they're supposed to be taking away from what they're looking at. Those who work with figures every day often forget that what to them seems simple and clear can look like gobbledygook to those of us without the relevant expertise.

The problems really kick in when you've got to roll out a data-heavy presentation to an audience who isn't used to dealing with that data. Here are some ideas on how to make it accessible to everyone, so that everyone gets what they need out of it.

- Have a *really* strong opening. You need to grab your audience, surprise them and challenge them. Think about some of the ideas we explored about openings in the chapter about openings. Don't open with a graph or chart, but open with something creative that starts to communicate the messages 'hidden' within the figures. I was working with an accounts team recently and they said the first thing they wanted their presentation to do was to explode the stereotype that accountants were dull. They ended up using everything from video to music and really made an impact.

  If you think your audience might be expecting you and your presentation to be a teensy bit dull, what are you going to do to blow those expectations out of the water right from the start?

- You need to explain very clearly what's in it for your audience. Why do they need to understand these figures? How will they benefit? Not just how will the business or organisation benefit, but how will they benefit as individuals if they take these figures on board? Will it make their job easier? Will they make more commission? Or will they understand why cuts are being made?

- Acknowledge early on that there are going to be lots of figures coming up, but never apologise for them, as that suggests that even you think they're dull. If you can't be passionate about this data and the messages it contains, why on earth should your audience be interested?

- Give them context. Why are these figures important to the team, department or organisation? How do they compare to historical figures? Where do they sit within the long-term goals or the values of the organisation? Context will really aid understanding.

- Don't just expect your audience to understand your graph or chart when you put it on a slide. Explain it and interpret it in simple but not simplistic language.

- Don't put full spreadsheets on a slide as they're hard enough for the presenter to read, let alone the audience, as each digit ends up being too small. If you need to present something like a cash flow forecast, profit and loss account or another big table, print it out and distribute it as a handout so people can see it up close. Ensure it is clearly titled.

- Make each slide count. Every graph, chart or table needs to serve a definite purpose and help you to tell your story and communicate your message. If you forgot to include this slide, would your audience still understand your message? If 'yes', drop the slide.

- Less is more, especially on a slide. Do you need to include every single piece of data you have in order to make the point you need to make?

For example, Figure 13 is a slide I saw while working with a big media buying agency in Manchester a couple of years ago.

Figure 13 A typical slide presenting data. Too much information presented to communicate the single point highlighted by the circle in the left column

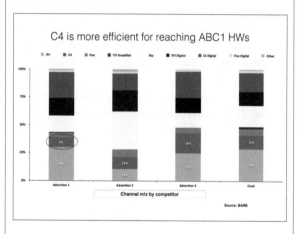

I asked the team using this slide what it needed to communicate to the client they were presenting it to. They pointed to the small circle on the left-hand column and said it was the fact that Channel 4 was 9 per cent more effective at reaching ABC1 High-Worth individuals. I asked them what the rest of the data was there for and they admitted that it wasn't relevant to this presentation, but that they wanted to show the client that they had done lots of research.

I pointed out that this seemed like an awful lot of unnecessary data to communicate just one fact. I asked them to go away and redesign the slide to make their main point clearer. They came back with Figure 14.

Figure 14 'Editorialising' the data makes the important point easier to understand and remember

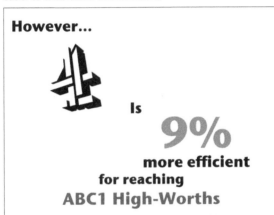

This to me is far more effective as a slide even though the design is unexciting. It's clear, easy to read and using the recognisable Channel 4 logo means we relate to it immediately. Also spelling out the word 'High-Worths' rather than using HWs makes it easier to understand. What they've done here is 'editorialise' the data, turning the important fact into a sentence or statement, making it far easier for them to communicate and far easier for the audience to understand. Other examples might be phrases like '75% of our customers like X while the remaining quarter like Y', rather than using yet another pie chart or bar chart.

When this revised slide was presented to the client, along with a handful of other similar slides (and the background data sent over in a PDF) the client commented that it was the first presentation this agency had given them that they'd really understood – a sobering moment for the agency staff.

Another lesson to be learned here is to 'cut to the chase'. The agency in the example above had been asking clients to put aside three hours for a 200-slide presentation, most of them graphs and charts. I challenged them to offer their five biggest clients an alternative – a 15 minute version with the background data sent over as a PDF.

Every single client opted for the 15-minute version and a couple even told the agency not to bother with the background data as 'we never read or understand it anyway'. Many audiences just want to know what the important data is and what they should do with it, that is: What decision do I need to make?

If you're not sure how much detail (and data) your audience or client wants, ask them. You might well be surprised by what they say. It doesn't mean they don't value your work and expertise, but they do value the fact that you respect their time and offer them a more concise, focused and practical alternative.

Some more ideas for presenting data:

- One of the ways to keep your audience interested in all the figures or data you need to present is to mix it up a little. More than two or three similar looking graphs on the trot will very quickly start to merge into one in the eyes of your audience.

Exercise

What different types of graphs and charts could you use in your next presentation? Could you editorialise some of your figures? Could you use an infographic (check out www.infogr.am for lots of great tools for creating them)? Could you find an image that highlights a particular number or trend?

- Find the story your figures are telling. Is it a positive story or negative story? Is there a challenge and resolution? Do the figures tell a story of heroism (someone making savings or bringing in more money) or villainy (a client failing to pay)? Do the figures tell of an impending tragedy – or do they point towards a farce? This isn't necessarily about telling a 'once upon a time' type story, but about describing the figures, their context and their effect in a more story-like way rather than just a list of numbers.

- Gamify it. Turn your presentation into a game. Ask people to predict where the figures have gone. Challenge them to a dual, a quiz, a game of snakes and ladders. Pass out the LEGO and ask them to build a bar chart to reflect the latest figures. Let them enjoy the figures and your delivery of them.

- Delivering bad news. Like all aspects of bringing a presentation to life, the way you choose to deliver your figures has to be context sensitive. If your figures are bad, you're probably not going to pass out the LEGO. Bad news doesn't have to be boring news, however. Acknowledge what the figures show (don't try to hide the key trends), but offer options, solutions and interpretations of causes. As someone who has expertise in data and figures, that expertise will be respected and required even more during times of crisis.

Getting ready to present

Thus far we've concentrated on your presentation, in other words, your content and how you're going to lay it out for your audience. Now let's turn to you, as the presenter, and how you are going to present. There's a lot to prepare before you take the stage.

Practical preparations

Let's start with some practical preparations you need to make in advance of your presentation.

First, find out as much as you can about where, when and how you're going to be presenting – and to whom. The more you know, the more confident and relaxed you can be. This list will vary depending on whether you're presenting in an internal meeting or at an external event, but some of the things I always try to find out include:

- What time am I presenting? I like to allow plenty of time to get there so I'm not panicking about being late. Time of day can also influence how receptive your audience will be. If you get an after lunch slot, for instance, you need to include plenty of engagement and interaction to keep your audience out of the post-lunch slump.

- How long am I presenting for? If you're given a specific length, make sure you stick to it. A great tool is an app called pClock on iOS or Presentation Clock on Android. It allows you to set a countdown timer that changes colour as you near the end of your time – and then starts counting up to show how much you're overrunning by. Time tends to go much faster than expected when presenting so don't just try to judge it as you go.

- To whom am I presenting? How many people? Who are they? How senior? What do they know about this topic already? What are they expecting? If you're not sure about these details, ask the person who asked you to present.

- What's the context of my presentation? Am I one of several speakers and if so, who is speaking before me and about what? (I will always try to watch anyone speaking before me in case what they say has a bearing on what I say.) Is it a meeting environment, a pitch or a conference style event?

- Where am I presenting? How do I get to the venue? What's the room like? How will the chairs be laid out – cabaret style, horseshoe or theatre style?

- What technology and other facilities will be available to me? Is there a projector or a plasma screen? What ratio does the screen work on? Can I run my slides from my own laptop or do I have to plug in to another computer?

- Do I need to provide my slides in advance? Are they planning to print them out and distribute them to delegates? (If they are, I'll produce a separate handout rather than distributing copies of the slides, for the reasons discussed previously.)

- Is there anything else that would be useful to know about this presentation? Why have they asked me as opposed to any other speaker?

Make a list of what you need to know before your next presentation.

Packing list

I also create a packing list in advance of a presentation, so I know what I need to take with me. The list will vary depending on my topic and the length of the presentation, but typically will include items such as:

- Laptop, power cable and projector connectors
- Clicker
- Cue cards or my outline of the presentation for last minute revision
- A USB stick with a copy of my slides (carried in a pocket in case I lose my bag)
- Flip chart and whiteboard pens
- Props I want to use
- Handouts for delegates
- Books I plan to mention and pass round
- Speakers if I'm using audio
- My business cards
- A couple of bottles of water (I prefer room temperature water)
- Mints
- Paracetamol (stuffy rooms give me a headache)
- A sheet with details of the venue, contact details for the person who booked me, travel arrangements and so on
- Feedback forms for delegates
- A spare shirt (I do have an awful habit of spilling coffee)

I now keep regular packing lists in Evernote, adding new items occasionally if I found I was missing something or something new was really useful.

Rehearsals

An actor would never go on stage without rehearsing. A lawyer would never stand up in court without rehearsing. A politician rehearses a conference speech many times over and Apple's Steve Jobs famously used to lock himself away for several days to rehearse his product keynotes (and if you're a fan of Jobs' presentations, check out the book about them in the resource list at the end of this book).

Yet many presenters don't bother rehearsing, preferring to 'busk' it. They spend hours honing what they want to say or creating slides, but then make an utter mess of delivering it, often because they've never said the words out loud.

Top tip

When you're planning your presentation, allow time to run through it at least twice before you put it in front of an audience, ideally more than that. Twice is the minimum because that allows you to try it once, make amendments and changes as necessary then try it again.

Two more top tips:

1. Video your rehearsal. You only need to prop up your smart-phone on a chair in the corner of the room to capture your

performance. Yes, we all hate watching ourselves on video, but it is the best way to understand how you come across to an audience. You'll immediately spot the long boring bits when there's not a lot going on. You'll spot the repetition or gaps in your content. You'll also spot any physical or verbal nervous tics such as fiddling with your glasses or always using certain words or phrases. I know I tend to append 'OK' to the end of sentences and overuse the word 'actually', but I only spotted these when I watched a video of a presentation I had given, which allowed me to start ironing them out. The first step to getting rid of these sorts of foibles is to be aware of them.

2 Rehearse in front of an audience – even just an audience of one. Get someone to critique both your presentation and your performance. Rehearsing in front of someone who doesn't know your area or topic that well (like your partner) can really help as they approach it as a layperson and can point out if you've failed to explain your points sufficiently. Rehearsing in front of your colleagues or peers is probably the hardest audience, as they'll know the topic as well as you and will be your harshest critics – but your presentation will be all the better as a result.

Dealing with nerves

There are whole books written on the topic of dealing with nerves, but it's a critical part of giving any presentation.

Some nerves are useful, essential in fact. They get the adrenaline pumping and will help keep you sharp and focused. Many people claim the adrenaline helps them to remember what they want to say. That adrenaline is what also gives you the 'high' of relief afterwards, and it's that high that those of us who enjoy presenting are probably addicted to.

I've been presenting in different forms for years, from school debates to stand-up gigs to business conferences, yet I still get some nerves before every single presentation, especially the major ones. If I didn't get nervous I'd be worried as that's when I might get complacent and not deliver my best. The trick is to take that nervous energy and focus it into your presentation.

Let's get one cliché out of the way right now. Do *not* try to imagine your audience naked. Who wants to picture their boss naked? How on earth is that meant to help?

To me there are four main steps in dealing with your nerves.

First, you need to recognise what it is that makes you nervous. Some people hate being the centre of attention, others are worried that all their expertise will desert them and they won't know what to say. The common thread for most people I work with is that they're nervous about looking stupid in front of an audience, especially an audience of people they know.

Second, you need to recognise how your nerves manifest or show. Do your hands shake? Do your legs turn to jelly? Do you get a dry throat or squeaky voice? Do you blush or sweat or does your mind go blank?

The third step is setting out to mitigate the factors in steps one and two. There's not a lot you can do about being the centre of attention when you're presenting, but maybe you could share the presenting with a colleague? It's also a case of getting used to it and even finding pride in the fact that people want to hear what you have to say. The more you do it, the easier it gets. If you're worried you are going to forget what you want to say, think about how you're going to guide yourself through your presentation. Cue cards with bullet points on them, for instance, mean you're only a glance away from knowing what to say next.

Mitigating against how your nerves manifest is a case of addressing your nervous response. If your hands shake use cue cards instead of paper notes, as cards shake less visibly. If your legs go to jelly, try stretching them and walking around before you go on, then practise standing with your feet shoulder width apart to give you a firm base.

Nerves tend to make people 'fold up' into unstable and uncomfortable positions, so practise unfolding yourself and finding a comfortable, confident position you can hold for a period of time. If you get a dry voice, have water to hand (and the slight pause to take a sip of water also gives you the chance to gather yourself and check your notes) or if you get a squeaky voice make sure you warm up beforehand (more on that shortly).

It is harder to stop a really physical response like sweating or blushing, but wear appropriate clothes that will help to minimise how visible it is. If you know your nerves are less likely to be visible to your audience, you'll be more relaxed and less nervous.

The fourth step to reducing your nerves is to prepare. Then prepare some more. Then rehearse and rehearse again. The more prepared you are, the less reason you have to be nervous. If you're worried about the questions you might be asked at the end of your presentation, make a list of likely questions and prepare some notes on how you would answer them. If you're worried you won't know the answer to a question, simply practise saying, 'I don't know that off the top of my head, but I'll check and come back to you later.' Job done.

Most nerves are actually about a fear of the unknown or unexpected. So it's completely within your power to know as much as possible and think through what to expect.

Exercise

Make a list of:

* What makes you nervous
* How your nerves manifest or show
* What you can do to address and reduce both what makes you nervous and how your nerves show

Warming up

Almost all professionals who use their voice and/or their body in their every day role will warm up before they start so they're limber, loose and ready to do the job without straining. This is exactly the same for a presenter.

Tips for warming up your voice

* Massage your cheeks, chin and neck to make sure your facial muscles are relaxed as these really impact how your voice sounds.

* Start warming up your vocal chords and resonance chambers by humming. 'Amazing Grace' is a great tune to hum as it has both high and low notes so will warm up the full range of your voice.

* Recite a few tongue twisters to get your lips, tongue and jaw moving. Try saying these a few times over, getting faster:

    o The lips, the teeth, the tip of the tongue
    o Red lorry, yellow lorry
    o Red leather, yellow leather

- Try to speak out loud in the minutes before your presentation, even just chatting to people as they arrive or talking in a meeting, so your voice is warm and ready.

- Even if you're sat in a meeting you can subtly do the facial massage and get your mouth moving. Perhaps don't sit there humming 'Amazing Grace' or reciting red lorry, yellow lorry as you might get some strange looks from your colleagues, but maybe excuse yourself to the toilet to warm up.

- Two tips on drinks – don't drink anything milky like a latte or hot chocolate before you present as these will coat your throat and make you sound less clear. Also try to drink room temperature water rather than chilled, both before and during your presentation, as chilled water will make your vocal chords contract and risks making your voice squeaky.

Tips for warming up your body

- Do some stretching, especially of your neck, shoulders and chest, to open up your chest so (a) you're breathing easily and (b) your arms and shoulders are ready to be mobile and expressive while you present. These don't need to be huge movements so you can do them while sitting in a meeting before you stand up to present to the room.

- Do some deep breathing to fill your lungs with air, especially if you're nervous. Practise slowing down your breathing by breathing in for a count of two then out for a count of two, then repeating for counts of four, six, eight and even ten. This doesn't mean gasping in the air then holding your breath for the count, but instead slowly taking in and then slowly expelling air from the full depth of your lungs over the duration of the count.

- If you're outside the room before presenting, you can be a bit more thorough with a physical warm-up. Some people need to jump up and down to energise themselves while others like to pace to burn off nervous energy. Try different things to find out what works for you.

What you're aiming for is a body and voice that is relaxed, looks and sounds confident and that doesn't betray any nerves. Yes, you might look (and sound) a bit odd doing some of these exercises, but believe me, they really do help.

A few other things to think about prior to your presentation:

- If there's an AV technician or team in the room you're presenting in, go and make friends with them as they can really help to make your presentation the best it can possibly be.

- Make sure you soundcheck beforehand. If there's a microphone on offer, use it as it takes the strain off your voice. Even if you're not using a mic, try to get on to the stage beforehand and practise how loud you'll need to speak to be heard at the back of the room.

- Make sure you go to the back of the room before the meeting or event starts. Have a look at where you'll be standing and notice how small you might be to those sat at the back. Do you need to make your volume louder and your body language bigger in order to make just as much of an impression on the people in the back row as on those in the front?

- Walk around the stage area (or patch of floor) to get used to how big it is and how much you can move without some people struggling to see you. Set everything up beforehand such as any props, flip chart and pens, your laptop, projector and so on so that when you're introduced or the event starts you can stand up and get on with it, not faff around (keeping everyone waiting) while you get sorted out.

All this preparation is important whether you're speaking in a meeting room at your office or a conference hall overseas. It's about being ready to present at your best by controlling and preparing yourself and your environment so you're focused, free from distractions and able to concentrate fully on your presentation and your audience.

Exercise

Make a list of all the things you need to do in order to prepare yourself for your next presentation. What do you need to do to be ready to present confidently and effectively?

90% of how well the talk will go is determined before the speaker steps on the platform.

Somers White

Presenting like a professional

I started this book by looking at what makes a great presentation and discussed the fact that it is as much about the person and how they present as it is about their content. Being asked to present should be taken as an honour and people giving you their attention and time is a privilege not to be taken lightly. Treat your audience with respect at all times and they'll return the accolade by listening to what you have to say.

This starts from the moment you 'take the stage', whether that's walking up the steps onto the platform and stepping up to the lectern or the front of the stage, or standing up in a meeting and moving to the front of the room.

Be confident. Be bold. Aim to create a strong first impression. People will be looking for you to fill them with confidence as you prepare to speak. Be in control (or at least appear to be, hence my advice on all that preparation in that last chapter); take your place; position yourself with your feet shoulder width apart and hands either by your side or in front of you; look around the room, let a smile play about your lips (unless you're about to deliver bad news, obviously); bring up your first slide if you're using them; take a good breath, and begin.

Know your opening words. Make them strong, loud if needed, but said with utter conviction. You know this. You've practised this. You're about to nail this.

And then all the preparation, planning, structuring and rehearsing pay off as you launch into your opening section.

But it doesn't all end there. As a presenter your job isn't just to deliver your presentation.

Stage presence

All the way through your presentation you need to be aware of a range of 'performance' factors that make up your stage presence.

Stage presence is the ability to attract and hold the attention of an audience. There is an element of charisma and energy involved, but that doesn't mean you're expected to be loud and larger than life, because someone quiet and intense can have just as much stage presence as someone big and loud.

Be aware of your energy level. A presenter needs to be operating on slightly elevated energy levels in terms of volume, animation and enthusiasm. If you stand in front of even quite a small roomful of people and talk as you would if you were holding a face-to-face conversation with one person, you'll come across as quiet and unengaged. This is one of the reasons warming up your voice and body is so important, so you're able to support them being used at a slightly higher level than usual.

Project your voice rather than shouting (practise this if it's not something you're used to) and let your body language and animated movement be bigger than usual, but don't turn into a caricature of yourself. Personally, if I'm speaking to up to about six people, I ramp myself up by about 20 per cent. If I'm speaking to up to 20 or so people, I'm me + 40 per cent. For big rooms and crowds, I'm probably nearer me with 70 per cent+ more energy and stage presence.

The other aspect that gives you stage presence is being relaxed and comfortable on a stage – or at least appearing to be. Let your body relax, let your movements be fluid and natural and smile as much as you can. If you seem to be enjoying yourself and your presentation, the audience is far more likely to enjoy it, too.

Build rapport

Rapport is the connection or relationship between presenter and audience and it's an important part of a successful presentation.

You build rapport in a number of ways and the process starts *before* you start your presentation.

- If you're in the room before your audience, greet them as they come in, shake hands, smile at them.

- If you walk into the room and your audience are already waiting, greet them warmly, show you're pleased to be there. If there aren't many of them, such as in a pitch meeting, shake hands with them all.

- You can even start building rapport before the day of the presentation by interacting with the people you're going to present to via social media, perhaps asking what they'd like to get out of your session.

- Humour is often a great way to develop rapport, but as discussed previously make sure it's appropriate to the context in which you're presenting. A humorous observation about the room, the weather or a very current news story can help to break down any barrier between 'me the presenter and you the audience' as it shows this is a shared space – we're all experiencing the same things.

- Once you're up and presenting, you continue to build rapport by using open body language (if you're not sure what that looks like, there are plenty of YouTube videos waiting to show you), making everyone feel included and connected to you.

- Eye contact is an important part of rapport. If you're in a meeting you do need to make sure you're making regular eye contact with everyone in the room. Don't just look at the most senior person in the room, the person who booked you or your best friend. If you're busy reading your slides or a script, you lose eye contact and thus rapport.

- If you're speaking to a large audience you can't make direct eye contact with everyone, so sweep your eyes across all sections of the audience regularly. It will feel to the audience members as if they're getting regular eye contact. Don't speak only to the front row – or the clock on the back wall.

- Even if it's the last thing you feel like doing – smile! We all respond warmly to a smile and it builds a really strong bond between audience and presenter.

Reading the room

A presenter must also read the room throughout the presentation. This means maintaining an awareness of the conditions in the room as well as the audience's mood and responsiveness. As the presenter you can take control of the room and if something is wrong, either ask for it to be fixed or do something about it yourself.

One of the factors you need to be aware of is the temperature in the room. A warm, stuffy room will send an audience into a stupor or off to sleep very fast. A cold room will see people wrap their arms or their clothes around themselves and will harden their mood. Watch for the clear signals like jumpers or jackets being taken off and people fanning themselves, or clothes being layered on and jackets being done up. Remember that you may be experiencing the room differently as you may be under a stage light or by a radiator, keeping you warm, or standing under the air conditioning unit.

If you think the temperature needs adjusting, check in with the audience on whether they're too hot or cold. Don't expect a consistent answer, though, as one person's 'too cold' is another person's 'just right'. Personally I think it's better for the room to be cooler rather than warmer to avoid the nodding heads as people fall asleep.

Top tip

You need to spot when you're losing people's attention. If they're more interested in checking their emails or what's going on out the window, you need to act fast to bring them back into the room. Run an exercise or ask a question or have some other form of interaction ready to refocus your audience.

Keep an eye out for light levels, too. A darkened room may help people see the slides better, but can also be soporific. If a room needs an energy boost, flooding it with light works well.

Be aware of the time of day you're presenting. After lunch is traditionally the 'graveyard' slot as people experience their after lunch slump, but last thing in the afternoon can also be hard as people are tired and have often seen enough. Presenting first thing in the morning can be tough as your audience may not be fully awake and functioning (are you?). Know how you're going to adjust to the time of day to make sure you can keep your audience with you.

So, as well as delivering your content, interacting with your audience, making sure the technology is working and bringing your presentation to life, you've also got to build rapport and read the room.

Sounds like a lot, but it's actually just one process. It's a set of activities that you probably do anyway, as we naturally look to see how a person we're speaking to is responding and adjust our behaviour accordingly. The more you do it, the easier it will get, until it becomes second-nature.

Stay in the moment

One of the commonest mistakes I see presenters (including some very experienced ones) make is not being 'in the moment'. By this I mean that they're not fully present on a moment-by-moment basis, but are detached and distracted, normally by their own script.

Speakers who aren't in the moment quite often take on that slightly sing-song delivery I mentioned in a previous chapter as they recite the script in their head out loud. They're not aware of what's going on in the room, but instead are just thinking of their next line or next slide. They often lose eye contact with their audience as they glance up or down as they aim to recall their next line.

It's one of the reasons why the most important piece of advice I can give to any speaker or presenter is, as I've already mentioned, 'Know what you want to say, but don't know your words'. With the exception of your opening line, as soon as you script something, you'll lose engagement because you become totally focused on the script and not on the audience.

Very experienced speakers can overcome this and reproduce the same scripted speech time after time while making it sound natural and off the cuff, but this takes years of practice. Personally I'd also find it a little dull and repetitive to say the same thing day in, day out, but it is *very* lucrative for some speakers.

Exercise

Return to the presentation you've worked on in previous chapters and think about the venue and the audience. Answer these questions:

- How much energy do I need to put into the room? Give yourself a percentage target. How will you achieve that? How will that feel?

- How will I build rapport with my audience? When will that process need to start?

- What do I need to look out for when I'm reading the room? What are the danger signs likely to be?

- How can I ensure I stay in the moment?

You can speak well if your tongue can
deliver the message of your heart.

John Ford

Putting it all into practice

In this book I set out to give you the tools, tips and skills you need to be a great presenter; to deliver with confidence, creativity and impact; and to meet your own objectives and those of your audience.

Hopefully you've now got plenty of ideas about how you can make your presentations stronger and more successful, and become a more accomplished presenter.

There's only one way to find out if your presentations and presenting skills are getting better: get out there and present. And present. And present again. The more regularly you present, the better you will get. Like any activity, it takes practice to build your confidence, both in yourself and in your newly honed skills.

Seek out opportunities to present. Ask to be sent out to present on behalf of your organisation. Volunteer to speak at meetings. Look for groups or events that might welcome or need a speaker on your area of expertise. Look for new areas of expertise or topics you could present on. Same skills, different content.

Always look for ways to improve your presenting. Ask for feedback from those in your audience, either in person or via a feedback form. Video your presentations, critique them and ask others to critique them, especially those you know to be good presenters themselves. Get some one-on-one presentation or speaker coaching, especially if you've got a make-or-break presentation coming up.

Top tip

People will be more honest if feedback can be given anonymously.

Look at the feedback and think about how you can address any issues that keep arising. As well as many groups that specialise in public speaking (details can be found in the appendix), look for complementary training and skill sets. Many years ago I did a stand-up comedy course that taught me so much, not only about using humour, but about how to write and structure content and how to speak in any room, to any audience. More recently I've been doing improv (improvised) comedy courses that have given me the confidence to relax on stage and think on my feet, knowing that just when I think I've got nothing to say, something vaguely relevant will come out of my mouth.

I know that I'm a good presenter, but I'm always looking to improve, to find new techniques and tools so that I can become a better presenter. I hope that this book has helped you become a better presenter too.

Appendix 1 Don't just take my word for it

Throughout this book I've made various assertions about what audiences do and don't like during presentations, especially around use of slides. Don't just take my word for it, however. While writing this book I undertook a piece of informal, totally unscientific research into the most common mistakes people see during business presentations (Figure 15). Having read this book, the results shouldn't come as any great surprise.

Figure 15 Common presentation mistakes: survey results

Cram too much information onto each slide	26 votes
Read their slides verbatim	23 votes
Have way too many slides	14 votes
(Other – see Figure 14)	11 votes
Rely on their slides to guide them through	10 votes
Read from a written script	8 votes
Overuse bullet points on slides	8 votes
Not keep to time and overrun their alloted slot	7 votes
Start with an apology	4 votes
Mumble their presentation	4 votes
Make little or no eye contact with the audience	4 votes
Use too many graphs or charts (that all look pretty much the same)	2 votes
Rush through it as fast as humany possible	1 vote
'Dance' from foot to foot or shuffle from foot to foot	1 vote

And for the sake of completeness, Figure 16 lists the 'other' mistakes.

Figure 16 'Other' presentation mistakes

'Show fear/nerves.'

'Endless repetition of filler words like 'uh' and 'you know' – completely distracting.'

'Rush the end.'

'You can't read this but...'

'Failing to explain the structure of the presentation – so we get a sequence of facts we can't organise – need to tell 'em what you'll tell 'em.'

'Too much text, not enough visuals.'

'Don't update slide from last presentation.'

'Incorrect room set-up/layout.'

'Not use a microphone – why do people always prefer to not use a microphone and shout instead?'

'Too much content.'

Have you fallen into any of these traps? Do you need to make sure you're not one of the presenters making these common mistakes? Keep this book to hand when you start preparing your next presentation.

Speech is power: speech is to persuade,
to convert, to compel.

Ralph Waldo Emerson

Appendix 2
Resources for becoming a better presenter

Books

Obviously you bought the best possible book about becoming a better presenter(!), but here are a few others I'd recommend checking out.

Atkinson, M. (2004) *Lend Me Your Ears*, Vermilion.

This book has been around for a few years and for good reason. The chapter on using rhetoric in speeches is brilliant and something I refer back to regularly.

Gallo, C. (2009) *The Presentation Secrets of Steve Jobs: How to be insanely great in front of any audience*, McGraw-Hill Education.

Dissects Jobs' Apple keynotes and contains lessons we can all learn on how to present. The chapter on delivering a 'holy shit moment' is particularly good.

Gibbins-Klein, M. and Schweikert, F. (eds) (2013) *The Business of Professional Speaking: Expert advice from top speakers to build your speaking career*, Panoma Press.

If you're interested in making speaking your profession and getting paid for it, this book of 14 essays by top speakers is a great resource for learning how to do so.

Jackson, L. (2013) *PowerPoint Surgery*, Engaging Books.

A very practical and business oriented look at producing great slides. Accessible and full of great tips. Recommended.

McCandless, D. (2012) *Information is Beautiful*, Collins.

Not actually about presentations, but about how to present data in beautiful and engaging ways.

Reynolds, G. (2011) *Presentation Zen*, New Riders.

Takes a design-led look at producing beautiful slides. Garr also has a terrific blog about presenting at www.presentationzen.com

Stevens, A. and du Toit, P. (2013) *The Exceptional Speaker*, Congruence Publishing.

The book you've just read has given you the basic and intermediate tools. This book, by two highly accomplished speakers, will help you become a more advanced speaker.

Groups and organisations

Toastmasters (www.toastmasters.org.uk)

A very well-established international organisation that has chapters and groups around the world running regular meetings specifically to help people become better speakers, whether you're delivering a business presentation or a best man's speech. Total disclosure: I've never been to one of their meetings, but I know dozens of people who rave about them, although there is definitely a Toastmasters 'house style' of speaking, which you can spot a mile off.

Professional Speaking Association (PSA) (www.thepsa.co.uk)

The 'trade body' for professional speakers and those who earn their living from speaking, including trainers, coaches, compères and many others. Runs regional meetings across the UK with the aim of helping members to 'Speak More, Speak Better'. If Toastmasters teaches you how to be a better speaker, the PSA teaches you how to get paid for it. They run an annual 'Speaker Factor' competition for new and upcoming speakers. I'm a Fellow of the PSA and was lucky enough to be named their UK Speaker of the Year in 2015. This organisation changed my business and my career for the better.

No one ever complains about a speech
being too short!

Ira Hayes

About the author

Steve Bustin is an award-winning keynote speaker, executive speech coach, presentation skills trainer and business communications consultant.

As a speaker, Steve delivers keynote speeches and breakout sessions on a range of communication and media topics including: presenting, PR and the media, social media and engaging communications. He speaks regularly at business conferences, mastermind groups and networking events in the UK and internationally.

Steve was named UK Speaker of the Year 2015 by the PSA and also won their London 'Speaker Factor' competition in 2013. He is a Fellow of the PSA and sits on the Board of the Association.

As a coach and mentor Steve works with business leaders to hone their speaking and presenting skills and position them as a go-to expert and speaker in their sector. He also trains teams in presentation skills, whether they're pitching to clients and prospects or speaking at internal meetings.

He ran PR consultancy Vada Media for 11 years, specialising in the health, medical and aesthetics sectors. He is the author of *The Authority Guide to PR for Small Business*, due Spring 2017.

Steve started his career as a Broadcast Journalist for BBC News and now writes for national magazines and newspapers, primarily on lifestyle, arts and gardening. He also regularly provides media interview training and coaching for those appearing in the media.

Steve lives in Brighton with his husband John, dog and chickens. He is a Trustee of Brighton Fringe, a Guest Lecturer in the Business School at The University of Brighton and a former Chairman of Seedy Sunday, the UK's largest community seed swap.

For more information visit stevebustin.com, follow @steveinbrighton on Twitter, connect with him on LinkedIn or contact him on steve@stevebustin.com

Also by Authority Guides

The Authority Guide to
Publishing Your Business Book:
Take your business to a new level by
becoming an authority in your field

Sue Richardson

Looking for a way to grow your business?

Publishing expert, Sue Richardson, shows you how to use your expertise,
knowledge and experience to become a published authority in your field
and gain the visibility you and your business needs. This Authority Guide
will help you to create a plan that ensures you write and publish the right
book for your business.

The Authority Guide to Marketing Your Business Book:
52 easy-to-follow tips from a book PR expert

Chantal Cooke

Want to get your business book flying off the shelves?

It's never too soon to start thinking about how to market and promote your book. In this Authority Guide, leading book PR and marketing expert Chantal Cooke, presents 52 tips that will make your book stand out from the crowd, build your credibility as an author, and ensure you achieve those all-important sales.